From

SHAME BREAKER

to

FULFILLMENT
TAKER

BREAKING THE SHAME OF YOUR
PAST TO TRANSFORM YOUR FUTURE

TONY CAIAZZA

**FEATURING THE AUTHOR'S POPULAR
SEMINAR MESSAGE "TRANSCENDING MINDSETS"**

From Shame Breaker to Fulfillment Taker
Breaking the Shame of Your
Past to Transform Your Future
by Tony Caiazza

Copyright ©2021 Tony Caiazza

Published by

Thirteen Twelve Publishing

Book design by Nick Zelinger, NZGraphics.com

ISBN: 978-1-7371901-0-3 (Print)

First Edition

Printed in the United States of America

To my Abba Father … it is you and only you.

To all the brokenness, hardships and disappointments; to every wound, mistake and regret; you have not become my kryptonite but rather succeeded to expose my superpower—Christ in me.

To my parents who somehow managed to overcome all the Herculean obstacles that could destroy even the best of us. You inspire my faith in the absolute power of God's restorative work that is available to all. Thank you for your story.

To my lovely wife, my biggest supporter for decades. You are my confidante and truest friend. I love you.

To my amazing daughter, for your patience and support. Your heart for those who have no voice inspires me. Because of you, I will keep striving to love and fight for those who can't do it for themselves. Keep being that voice to this generation.

To all the spiritual mothers and fathers who imparted within me wisdom and spiritual gifts to be who I am today, and to my church family at the International Church of Las Vegas (ICLV) where this journey began.

To all who helped with completing my first book:
Karina Garrison, Chris Ford, Rick Bolesta.
Each of you gave the most important commodity
in life … your time.

Contents

Introduction

Imagine if you could start fresh again by pressing the reset button of your life. Think about that concept a moment. Every mistake, trial and failure that's chained your soul with shame would become powerless to continue to dictate your identity. What an incredible visualization.

That is what the "reset button" does. It resets a person's understanding by erasing the accusing graffiti that has covered his or her soul from the truth—the truth that he or she is someone who *matters*, someone who has been wonderfully made with purpose and love.

Envision how your life would change if you were set free from shame—if you evicted it from every dark corner of your being. What if you could empty your mind and emotions of all the false agreements you have believed from this world—warped understandings rooted in an onslaught of negative messages about who you are and what brings lasting fulfillment? What then? Would you be willing at last to open your mind to find a healthier way to obtain self-worth and fulfillment? And if so, how would you go about finding that miraculous reset button of your life?

Well, this book may help you. Two thousand years ago, a revolutionary message was brought to the world. It was the biggest reset button humanity has ever had or ever will encounter.

This book is not about religion or some of its distorted notions. Instead, this book is about spiritual awakening and experiencing the tangible, supernatural, finished work of Jesus Christ—the kind of finished work that *transforms* and *restores* a person through personal experience, identification and recovered self-worth.

From Shame Breaker to Fulfillment Taker is written with a fresh perspective on how to overcome the shame of a person's past and reach for the God-given potential in his or her life. It helps navigate a person to do this by experiencing the purest relationship source possible: Jesus.

Remember that God is in the fulfillment business and He leaves nothing incomplete. That includes you.

Recognize There is More

*"The depth of our hunger for God will determine
the depth of our filling."*
~ Anonymous

In her book, *Presence*, Harvard Business School Professor Amy Cuddy describes how, when we meet someone for the first time, subconsciously, we think two things during the greeting phase. "Can I trust you?" and "Can I respect you?" In many ways, a book follows suit. That's why it's important not to skip the introduction of this book. The intro is intended to build a solid foundation of trust and respect, which are required for this journey of becoming a Shame Breaker and Fulfillment Maker. I guarantee that turning back now to read the introduction of this book, if you haven't already done so, will be well worth the effort. Once you complete the intro, cruise ahead to "There Is More."

~ There Is More

On a damp Fall morning back in 2000, I was just starting my first year of Masters Commission, a discipleship training program designed to equip young people for full-time ministry. I joined at a much older age than the other students. I was 29 and had already lived slam-packed with life lessons from the world-renowned school of hard knocks. Some of you may have gone to this same school and know what I mean. For those of you who don't, it's an education not found in any classroom, but rather an education with firsthand experiences of consequences that bad choices bring. I desperately tried to hide those years from everyone, especially the other students, most of whom joined the program immediately after high school. Since I was older, I was tasked with driving the 15-passenger van from our home church in Las Vegas to several churches in the beautiful Pacific Northwest. It was my first time out on the open road and I was excited to begin this new chapter of my life.

Up to this point, I felt deeply unsatisfied in my heart. Something was missing. Nothing I was learning and experiencing seemed fulfilling, though I didn't understand why. Now I know: Shame from my past had left me feeling unfulfilled and desperately wanting more of God. I would place my head on my pillow at night, sigh, and say, "Is this it Lord? Is something wrong with me? There must be more."

I remember having one of those conversations with God the night before preaching for the first time. Except, the next morning, I awoke feeling completely different. God, I realized, had visited me during the night. His presence was all over me. I couldn't remember details about what, exactly, happened during the night except that it was the best night's sleep I'd ever had, despite it being on a hardwood floor.

I got dressed, loaded the musical instruments, and gathered the students into the van while quickly skimming my sermon notes on Psalm 42:1-5: "As the deer thirsts for the water so my soul thirsts for God." Then something supernatural happened. I pulled the van in front of the small church. Everyone rushed out with their Bibles and instruments in tow. I stayed back to say a quick prayer for help in delivering my first sermon. As I reached to pull the keys from the ignition, a droplet of morning dew on the windshield caught my eye. Springing from it was a light that grew brighter and brighter, somehow pulling me into it as though it were some sort of portal to another dimension. As I came face to face with this bright light, I could sense right away (without any need for introduction) it was Jesus.

His presence declared who he was and every cell within me responded with an intense awareness. I also recognized this was the same presence I had felt the previous night. Immediately, something happened within a deep place inside of me—a place I didn't even know existed—transforming my life forever. I looked at his face. It was bright light and his hair and beard glistened like many droplets of oil, reflecting more brilliantly than any diamond. His eyes were like the deepest water that you could so easily get lost in. I couldn't tell what he was wearing because the light coming from his upper body was so bright and intense that it was all I could see.

His light was like rays that moved and touched all things. As these rays of light hit me, I became over-whelmed because I could feel his power flowing from within this light. It was overtaking the deepest parts of me and no part of me could hide from it. I some-how knew he was strengthening me to withstand his brilliance.

This power was beyond my ability to describe. I remember thinking, "Nothing could possibly be more powerful than he." It was not like he was showing off; it was simply who he was. At that moment, I realized that my own body was glowing. I was being charged and flooded with light and an awareness that all created things were, somehow, connected to him.

An all-consuming love flowed from him. This love was so strong that my only desire was to stay close to him. Somehow, I knew I was made of his light and that he is the true light … that all things seen and unseen are made of him and his wonderful light. Just as John states in the opening chapter of his Gospel, Jesus is the light of the world and he freely shares his light with us, even though this world doesn't recognize or receive it.

Immediately, I knew Jesus was one with the Father and that everything that exists is connected to them both. Jesus' light is the messenger of all life and contains all revelation. My vulnerabilities (the things I once so desperately hid from the world) could not hide from his loving light. With gratitude, I recognized that he was embracing all my flaws like a comforting hug gently enveloping me and accepting me as I truly was. Intuitively, I knew that, without this light, no life could exist. And, suddenly, I also knew that all life hinges completely on God's living light.

From time to time as I pray, I can still see the light of Jesus connecting to everything. This love is hard to describe because it cannot be quantified. What I can say with certainty is this: It in no way casts shame upon others because it penetrates our vulnerabilities with absolute love, creating his strength from our weakness.

This experience changed my life and ministry dramatically. I know there is absolutely nothing more powerful and mighty than Jesus. So many of us feel as if we've failed too greatly ever to be accepted into God's perfect light. But I assure you, it is already shining on you if you'll just accept it. Today, as a middle-aged man, I look back on this experience with better understanding. I know now that, no matter your choices or traumas, God is always available to heal you and bring you into a place of fulfillment. His light that connects us all should be seen and honored in everyone around us.

We all have stories of shame in our lives, leading us to hide parts of ourselves from the world. But it's time we shine the light of Jesus Christ onto the pages of those shame stories. There is so much available to us if we're willing to believe and receive. My supernatural encounter with Jesus helped me appreciate 2 Corinthians 3:17 in a new way: Where the spirit of the Lord is, there is freedom—freedom from the chains of shame and everything destructive connected to it. My mission is to proclaim this freedom-activating power to whomever God leads me, and I believe that includes *you*. With that in mind, we're now ready to begin our journey of shame breaking and fulfillment taking!

~ **Prayer for More** ~

Let's pray together for understanding and insight to know Christ more deeply than ever before. You are not alone in this prayer. Many others have joined with you in reading it. The first step into becoming a Shame Breaker and Fulfillment Maker is asking for more of Christ:

Jesus, I want to connect with you more than ever before. Come into every part of me and reset my understanding of you. Clear from the table of my mind, will, and emotions anything that is not from you. I want to "taste and see" that you are good. Open the blueprints of your Kingdom within me and build me up in your mercy and grace. Thank you for your mercy and grace. I receive them as your free gifts. I reject every destructive force that is at work against me, in the powerful name and blood of Jesus Christ.

Please, Lord, lead me into the perfect fulfillment you have for me. Lead me into your presence so deeply that I cast off everything that entangles me and keeps me from experiencing you. Help me see that, through your mighty love and power, I am free to be filled—and fulfilled—by You. In Jesus' matchless name.

Amen.

Your Identity Shapes Your Reality

"There are three persons living in each of us: the one we think we are, the one other people think we are, and the one God knows we are."
~ Leonard Ravenhill

The way we identify with ourselves is the most important aspect to living a fulfilled life. Everything flows from this spectacular place called self. We as Christians, at times, can be critical of the idea of self, viewing self-love negatively and twisting it into a New Age belief system that distorts the true beauty of how God views us. This skewed perspective creates a source of intense shame, trapping Christians and preventing them from living in the victory of Christ's finished work on the cross. Our view of self forms the core of how we treat ourselves and how we treat others. We are far from ugly. It is the sin within that is ugly. **Yet, somehow, we manage to kick ourselves and each other rather than kicking the sin.**

Carefully consider Psalm 139:14 (NIV), "I praise you because I am fearfully and wonderfully made; your works are wonderful, I know that full well." Please receive this wonderful scriptural truth. You, right now, are wonderful. You are the wonderful work of the master craftsman, the one living God. The word "fearfully" means "awestruck" and "reverenced." This passage is saying you are awestruck, reverenced, and wonderfully made.

Stop and think about that. Think hard on this passage. Read it a few times. Take a moment and praise God that you are wonderful. He made you wonderful! Now, look at yourself in the mirror and tell yourself you are wonderful. Yes, right now, please put this book down and look in the mirror and tell yourself you are wonderful! Don't read further until you do this.

Notice what happened as you tried this simple exercise. How did it feel? Uneasy? Uncomfortable? Did it seem fake? Did guilt and memories of mistakes and mistreatments surface? Did you somehow feel it was wrong to say affirming words to yourself because you were brought up thinking you are unworthy of such claims? Many of us have a very difficult time doing this exercise because our reflection doesn't match the words "I am wonderful." We do not respect ourselves (or God, who created us) as being his wonderfully made creation. But being wonderful does not mean you are perfect or somehow unflawed.

On the contrary, we are all flawed and imperfect. Yet, in some part of God's miraculous plan, He calls you wonderful and desires to unfold the mysteries of Christ by working within your imperfections. Embracing God's love and acceptance through the supernatural work of Jesus Christ is the unfolding mystery of your story. **Your imperfections speak volumes about your worth through God's eyes.** What a lie humanity embraces if we think we must attain perfection to be accepted by God. Fearful of being rejected, we shield our weaknesses from everyone, suiting up with the wrong armor. Hiding inside it, we're terrified that, if others figured out exactly who we really are, they'd reject us. We live in this false armor at work, at school, and at church—day after day, month after month, and year after year. We wear this false armor so long and often that it becomes difficult to remove, even when we're around our spouse, our children, and even ourselves. The fear of not fitting in and being truly accepted can rob every aspect of life.

When we fail to see Christ's marvelous light in ourselves and others, the lens of how we view everything else becomes distorted. How we see ourselves must be confronted now, at the very beginning of this journey, as it effects our lives so powerfully. The way we view ourselves is the way we view our world. As evidence, consider the tale of two dogs.

~ The Tale of Two Dogs

Two dogs, at separate times, enter the same room. One exits wagging its tail while the other comes out growling. A woman watching the proceedings goes into the room to see what could have possibly made one dog so happy and the other so mad. To her surprise, she finds a room filled with mirrors. The happy dog found a thousand happy dogs looking back at him while the angry dog saw only angry dogs growling back at him.

What you see in the world around you reflects how you see yourself. When God is your mirror, you begin to see things from a fresh, new perspective. It is my prayer that you see yourself through the reflection of God's mirror and not the culture of this world.

~ Prayer ~

Father, I ask that you open my eyes to view myself as you truly see me. Remove the things that obstruct my vision of how you think and feel about me. Please help me to love and accept myself the way you love and accept me. I affirm that I am fearfully and wonderfully made by you and precious in your sight. In the power of Jesus' name, I break off my life all lies that tell me I am not worthy of love. Father, fill me with your eyesight when I look at myself. Give me fresh eyes to see how you view me and how you love me.

Amen.

Your Wonderful Mind

"If you believe you can, you probably can.
If you believe you won't, you most assuredly won't.
Belief is the ignition switch that gets you off
the launching pad."
~ Denis Waitley

You live in the reality of what lives inside your mind. If you change what lives inside, you will change your whole world. This principle is precisely related to how you view yourself. The mind is the compass that guides us through every moment of our existence, shaping and formulating opinions of how we see ourselves and others along the way. It's an extraordinary creation and, from it, virtually anything is possible. Your fulfillment hinges upon this very source. It's been said, "Whatever the mind can conceive and believe, it can achieve." What a powerful statement! From the mind, we imagine situations and outcomes continuously.

At work within us every second of every day, the mind never stops. It's a continuous motor that never shuts off, 24/7. When you're awake, it imagines and when you're sleeping, it dreams. As humans, we imagine and dream all the time. The innerworkings of our mind are an endless source of creativity that can be used as a powerful tool for good or evil. Which explains why the Enemy of Our Soul uses the mind to wage war against us.

~ Where the Head Goes the Body Goes

"The thief comes only to steal and kill and destroy;
I have come that they may have life and have it
to the full."
— (John 10:10, NIV).

Your mind represents the front line in the battle for your personal fulfillment. It has no autopilot or cruise control. In fact, it's the only part of you that has free will. The mind has the innate ability to make choices that produce how we think, feel, and act. Think of it as the control station for your fulfillment.

I have had great opportunities over the years to train in martial arts with some of the best teachers in the world. One teacher taught me several techniques for controlling and manipulating my opponent's body and tossing it off balance. The method consisted of a series of quick moves to coax my opponent to drop his guard from protecting his head. To execute the technique, I'd create a distraction then quickly grab my opponent's head, twisting and turning it in whatever direction I desired. This exercise powerfully illustrated a martial arts maxim: "Where the head goes, the body goes."

In the same way, Satan, the Enemy of Your Soul, is always trying to draw you off guard in order to turn your head and toss you off balance. Dark powers constantly are at work to distract you, preventing you from obtaining the fulfillment God desires for your life. The war of the mind starts in the imaginations and dreams of what you *think* will make you feel fulfilled. Your mind has been under attack since the beginning of your existence. As you learn to understand and recognize its point of entry and its strategies, you will be better equipped to battle this foe and overcome in Jesus' name.

~ The Mind Trap of a Worldly Culture

Take a moment to ponder this: For countless generations before you were born, humanity, in its flawed and fear-filled state, produced a massive vision. For the purposes of this book, I will refer to this vision as the "worldly culture" view. This view is formed from a collection of generational visions of government, family, education, business and finance, entertainment, media, technology, and even religion.

Combined, these forces create the most influential vision of humanity. Over the years, many have referred to them as "gates of influence" or "mountains of influence." Regardless of the name, they are the strategies of a worldly culture and they embody all of society's rules, beliefs, and laws, as well as what it worships.

The vision of humanity is not all bad. Some wonderful things have come from it. But it also has so many traps and pressures that entice us to conform to the image of the dark spiritual forces that distort the truth of Christ in humanity, and block our fulfillment. I call this, "on earth as it is in hell." As you continue reading this book, I pray you'll experience many aha! moments that will uncover Satan's cunning strategies.

The subtle scheme of producing shame on Earth begins as we unconsciously form agreements with the people who set in motion belief systems long before we were born. There are belief systems that have been set in motion with such force and momentum that it reminds me of a mighty river. We are caught into the beliefs of our own people groups. We are pulled in due to the need to acquire self-esteem. We do this by living up to specific values that are prescribed by the people group we are part of. Every one of us is vulnerable to thinking that the ideas we hold dear are rational or upright positions, but how many of our ideas are adopted and defended as part of our tribal identity? Think about it ... Racism of all types is bread from a belief system that says anyone who is different from my tribe is dehumanized. Nobody deserves to be treated less than human, yet to varying degrees we minimize others worth in our eyes if they don't look like us, make money like us, are smart like us, worship like us, speak our language like us, or even vote like us. We form agreements against them and unfortunately against ourselves and God who made us. When our self-worth is based on conformity to the ideas of our tribe as the standard to what is right, we set ourselves up for shame in our lives.

These ideas have created generational agreements that have formed invisible soul ties to nations, families, and even to our churches. As children, we didn't have the opportunity to choose our beliefs. Instead, we agreed with the information that was passed to us from the culture of this world. It is impossible to be free from these entanglements because they have become part of our nature—a nature marred by sin, which simply means missing the mark of God's perfect standard. Our sin nature is why Jesus said we must be "born again," referring to a spiritual birth. In John, Chapter 3, he went on to explain that, if we're not born both of water (referring to the amniotic fluid of human birth) and of the spirit (referring to spiritual birth), we "cannot enter the kingdom of God" (John

3:5). It is impossible to understand how tied we are to this worldly culture influence without the Holy Spirit working within us to see this truth.

"The person without the Spirit does not accept the things that come from the Spirit of God but considers them foolishness and cannot understand them because they are discerned only through the Spirit" — 1 Corinthians 2:14 (NIV).

~ Prayer ~

Lord, You are my strength, my rock, my fortress and my deliverer. I make the choice to take refuge in you. You Jesus, are my shield and my salvation. I ask that You break the forces at work against me in this world. The forces that try to capture my mind from living within Your best for my life. Silence and scatter every generational lie. Holy Spirit, lead me into your truth, expose every lie and every deception that holds me back from your best. Deliver me and rescue me from the culture of this world. I want to be filled with your Spirit and live in the light of Your truth and love.

Amen.

Our Spiritual Backpacks and the Stones of Shame

"Do not let your shadow walk you. You are not a slave to the past. So today instead of regretting where you have been ... give thanks for where you are going!"
~ Sean Smith

We have been programmed to view everything we see through the filter of our worldly culture and our experiences. In this context, we begin to form beliefs and judgments and make binding agreements within ourselves about who we are and the people around us. We carry these agreements in our hearts.

Think of your soul as your spiritual backpack. These backpacks are made of our mind, will, and emotions, and they affect the health of our bodies. Our backpacks are the essence of who we are. What we carry with us in these backpacks (our souls) affects our whole being. As humans, we are continually on a scavenger hunt, choosing what to put in our packs and even filling others' packs as well. We can place helpful things in them and propel ourselves to greater fulfillment or we can put harmful things in that cripple us.

We cannot control what life tosses our way but we always have control over what we allow into our backpacks from our experiences. A spiritual battle is continually being fought to determine what we hold within our pack. If we're not careful, we risk becoming like a puppet with our soul tied to the destructive Puppet Master, constantly at work on the stage of this worldly culture. As our soul becomes tied to worldly influence, the Puppet Master manipulates our strings like a marionette. Increasingly, we play the role of the accuser and judge, limping through life with backpacks laden with heavy stones of shame. As we judge ourselves, we shovel more heavy shame stones into our packs until we're crippled by the unbearable weight. All the while, we heap stones of accusation and judgment into other people's packs, as well, assuming that burdening others will somehow relieve our own intolerable load. But, in reality, it only makes things worse.

Many committed Christians have been paralyzed because of this manipulation. Or, if not paralyzed, badly battered by the shame stones they sling at one another. But how did we get to this place? Just as our government has laws that manage society's ideas of fulfillment through right and wrong, our internal belief system also has laws that manage our personal fulfillment. All these laws exist in our mind. We believe in them so strongly that they become the center of our reasoning. And when we feel these laws are broken, the accuser and judge inside us takes action.

As our internal critic points the finger and pronounces guilty verdicts, we, in turn, suffer the resulting guilt and punishment. We call this process justice and somehow feel gratified knowing that punishment has been meted out and justice has been served. But was it really? True justice is paying only one time for a mistake. Injustice is the unfairness of paying more than once for each mistake. Jesus paid the price once and for all for our mistakes that is the beauty of God's love (Romans 6:10-11). In our legal system, being prosecuted more than once for the same offense is called "double jeopardy" and it's prohibited.

Answer this question. How many times do you pay for the same mistake? For many of us, we punish and shame ourselves over and over again. We stone ourselves with shame each time we replay a humiliating event in our mind. We can be having a wonderful day where everything is going great—the birds are chirping, the sun is out, there's not a care in the world. Then, suddenly, something triggers a shame event inside us. We replay the scene over and over like an old TV rerun, each time condemning ourselves. **Humanity is the only creation on earth that pays many times over for the same mistake.** This is an extremely toxic cycle, a revolving wheel that dishes out shame continuously.

The cycle looks like this:

Step 1. We make a mistake.

Step 2. We assign blame.

Step 3. We judge ourselves and issue a guilty verdict.

Step 4. We stone ourselves with shame as punishment.

Step 5. We repeat this process every time we think about the mistake.

If we truly desire justice, then one punishment per crime is enough. But if our minds are trapped in shame, each time we remember a wrongdoing, we judge ourselves again. We issue a guilty verdict again and we issue punishment again, and again, and again. Is that justice? No. That is unfair. In fact, it is torment.

This harmful practice is based on a flawed law created by the accuser, himself. Satan is the chief finger pointer and ridiculer of your wonderful, flawed self. He acts as a wall, a blind spot, preventing you from understanding how God sees you. Many of the beliefs cemented in our minds are nothing but lies, and we suffer because we believe and participate in spreading them. John 8:44 tells us that Satan is the "father of lies." It is time to reject him and pardon yourself from the mistakes of your past. After all, God already has done just that.

As I write this, I know some of you have made mistakes you cannot let go of. You are punishing yourself repeatedly. The stones of shame are weighing you down. Now—right now—is the time to stop carrying those stones and let the Lord empty your pack! The load you carry is not from God. It is a lie meant to keep you tormented and robbed of experiencing the fulfilled life God desires you to have. Nothing will block the stones of shame from pummeling your life more than your decision to recognize, believe, and internalize the fact that Jesus paid the price and took the punishment for you, providing the absolute, once-and-for-all, finished work of the cross. The last words from his last breath on that cross were, "It is finished." Now the question is: Are you finished— finished carrying your heavy load of shame?

"Come to me, all you who are weary and burdened, and I will give you rest. Take my yoke upon you and learn from me, for I am gentle and humble in heart, and you will find rest for your souls. For my yoke is easy and my burden is light" — (Matthew 11:28-30, NIV).

~ **Prayer** ~

Lord Jesus, help me to remove the heavy stones I carry. The weight of shame I carry is just too much, and I need your help. I thank you that I can find rest in your presence. I accept your loving peace in my life. I reject and let go of every heavy shame accusation that has been thrown at me by this world and myself. Give me strength to forgive those that have hurt me and bring your healing touch to my life. I ask you to please forgive me for any stones I have set on myself and others. I choose now to drop those stones of shame and be free.

Amen.

The Soil of Our Minds, the Seeds of Our Words

*"Words are invisible, but if misused,
can prove deadly."*
~ Lisa Bevere

Your mind is fantastically fertile. In fact, the mind is more fertile than any soil on earth. It can produce any crop it chooses. Each day, seeds are continually dropped onto the soil of your mind. The seeds are opinions, theories, and beliefs—mixed, if you're fortunate, with truth—expressed through words. You see, words are like powerful seeds. Each one contains a little bit of the life force of those opinions, theories, beliefs, or truths behind them; and each seed has the power to bear good fruit or bad fruit. Each seed can be either healthy and life-giving or toxic and death-dealing.

Proverbs 18:21 (AMP) explains the phenomenon this way: "Death and life are in the power of the tongue, and those who love it and indulge it will eat its fruit and bear the consequences of their words." It's essential to know what kind of seeds our minds like to fall in love with and indulge. Are we reaping the consequences of good fruit, allowing, as Galatians 5:22-23 says, "love, joy, peace, patience, kindness, goodness, faithfulness, gentleness and self-control" to take root?

These good fruits are the produce of the Holy Spirit at work within us, bringing about blessings and fulfillment. In the same way, the consequences of bad fruit from evil spirits are hate, sadness, conflict, impatience, envy, cruelty, unfaithfulness, harshness, and self-destructiveness. This type of fruit produces cursing and unfulfillment on our lives. The question is: what consequences—what fruit—are we producing? Inside every person is a conjurer, and we can either put a curse on someone with our words or we can send blessing and set people free. We cast conjuring every day all the time with our opinions, theories, and beliefs. Let me give you an example.

I know a dad who was a smart man and had good intentions to do what was right for his family. This father loved his son very much. One night, the dad came home from a very bad day at the office after running behind on his presentation that was due the next morning. Exhausted and stressed, the last thing he wanted was a briefcase full of work to do after hours, though that's exactly what he brought home with him. Hoping for peace and quiet so he could complete his work quickly, instead he encountered his rambunctious young son, Brian.

The boy had spent hours earlier that day making a sword out of leftover cardboard. Brimming with creativity, he'd used masking tape and colored markers to fashion a bright blue blade and a twisted brown handle. Once the sword was complete, Brian began running and jumping happily, brandishing his masterpiece. "Dad, Dad! Hey, Dad! Look at my new sword," he whooped, as his father entered the front door, oblivious to his anxiety.

Brian was lost in his own world of exciting, creative imagination. Feeling brave, strong and skilled, he imagined beating up bad guys with his new weapon. "Swoosh! Take that, Mr. Mean Man!" he shouted as he pretended to kick the bad guy. Brian jumped wildly and shouted louder and louder, expressing his pleasure and confidence at being brave, strong, and creative. Snapping from the sensory overload, Brian's father erupted. He scowled at the innocent little boy and yelled, "Shut the hell up! That's just stupid paper and you're no superhero! You're just a weak little kid! Just stop it! Now sit down, be quiet, and go watch TV!"

Tearing the sword from Brian's little hands, the father tossed it to the ground saying, "And go put this mess in the trash before your mother comes home!"

In reality, the son wasn't weak and uncreative; the father's patience for any distraction was simply non-existent. Even so, Brian believed his dad's belittling words. This type of outburst had happened a handful of times before and, as a result, Brian made an agreement with himself: "I am weak and in the way, and I am no good at art." As a result, Brian soon grew shy at school. If he was asked to play sports or do any type of art project, he refused. Anything that required strength or creativity was difficult. Even talking to others became a challenge. Everything changed inside this little boy because of the agreement he'd made in his mind. He believed he had to hide his authentic self in order to be accepted and loved.

The world around us always attempts to typecast who we are. To demonstrate this concept, I once took a jar of pasta sauce, removed its label, and replaced it with a peanut-butter-jar label. I was preaching at a youth camp and passed the jar around for everyone to examine. One by one, each person laughed as they held it in their hand and said, "That's not peanut butter! That's spaghetti sauce!"

They all noticed right away that what was on the inside didn't match what was on the label. In the same way, **many of us are experiencing an identity crisis. We wear a label out in the world that doesn't reflect who we truly are.** We've allowed external, negative forces to re-label us. Just as every label contains an ingredients list, we, too, make unconscious agreements based on someone else's opinion about what we're made of. Whenever we hear an opinion and believe it, we make an agreement and it becomes part of our belief system. Brian grew up and, even though the ingredients inside him were strong, brave, and creative, he never had confidence for group activities. He developed an emotionally crippling complex from one conjuring of a seed of bad fruit sent his way. Or, put another way, he carried a heavy stone in his spiritual backpack. This stone, or bad seed, was cast upon him by the one he loved and trusted, his own father.

Creativity and spiritual giftedness are powerful forces given to us by God. The Enemy of Our Souls has always used shame as an instrument to keep our gifts locked deep inside. Many times in my own life, as I stepped out in my God-given gifts for the purpose of revealing and glorifying God, I have been attacked with shame. **Shame makes us feel small, which can lead us to hide the very power that God has paid the highest price to give us.**

For example, many years ago, while attending ministry school in a large Las Vegas church, I was asked to participate in the Sunday service prayer ministry. I had always known that God had given me the desire and gifting to pray for people. I loved it and, to me, there was nothing more satisfying than partnering with the Holy Spirit to serve others in prayer. I remember during those years the desire to press into God and ask for spiritual gifts. I fasted and prayed that I would increase in God's love and I noted, in writing, the gifts of the Spirit that I desired to function in, drawing from the list in 1 Corinthians 14.

One of the first experiences I had involving this phenomenon occurred at a San Diego youth camp. Several youth groups were attending the camp and I was asked to pray with the students as they came forward. That night, as the speaker issued the call to Salvation, over a hundred youth came forward for prayer. At that moment, just like in Rev 3:20, I saw a wooden double door. The door was closed and it had no door knob on the side I was facing. I understood immediately that the only way the door could be opened was from the other side and Jesus wanted to enter through that door. He was waiting for the person to open the door and invite him in from their side.

I was actually seeing the door of each person's heart as if I was standing in front of it. Each time I prayed for a person, I explained to them what I was seeing. I told them God was inviting them to open the door of their heart from their side and let Christ in. When they opened the door, I saw light flood inside the doorway and enter into each person. This light was a flood of Christ's love. It was Jesus entering inside the heart of each person—a lovely, living, light of life. It was so powerful and yet loving beyond words.

As each person opened the door and Christ entered in, they all would fall to the ground (though not from a heavy-handed push like you sometimes see on TV). No, this was all Jesus, fully displaying his love and power to each person. It was motivating to see each person have a life-changing encounter with the Lord. People were weeping with joy and filled with love and hope beyond measure. (This supernatural filling still happens at altar invitations and I am always eager to accept when God calls me to participate.)

It's amazing how God desires to use us as his instruments to reveal salvation. As I prayed for others, I began to see what I can only describe as a quick image of things I believed God wanted me to pray. As these quick mental images would enter my mind, I would pray aloud what I had seen.

Even so, it hasn't always been easy and it didn't take long after my experience at the youth camp to get attacked by shame for operating in this spiritual gift. I remember volunteering in another youth ministry and, during a time of worship, I began to pray with a student. The Holy Spirit began to touch people, one by one. It was a beautiful moment and I recognized that God was desiring to move in a great way in the lives of these young people. Manifestations of the Spirit's presence and power began to happen at nearly every gathering we hosted.

One morning, however, immediately after the service, I was pulled aside by one of the church leaders. He suggested that I was using the altar ministry to call attention to myself and he reminded me that he, not I, was in charge of the ministry. I was taken back at the thought that I was somehow being perceived as taking over and seeking attention. "Could it be?" I wondered. "Was I wrong in praying for others when they asked for it?" I was deeply wounded and not mature enough to talk with others who could counsel me on how to respond and grow from this rebuke.

Before long, I began to feel rejected and angry. My shame trigger had been activated and I quickly pulled away from helping out in that ministry or with that particular leader again.

Many years later, looking back, I know it was the Enemy creating division in the ranks. Often, when it comes to spiritual giftedness and creativity, many of us have been wounded by our peers or leaders. Incidents like the one I described can cause us to hold back and hide and, in some cases, become bitter and backslide away from the fulfillment of God's best for our life. Nothing will make God's people more ineffective than shame. Shame takes an axe to the root of our creativity and individuality. The giftedness and creativity of God in us is part of the light He desires to display to this world.

To this day, I am always challenged to stay in the realm of what is comfortable and play it safe. I find, in certain environments, I'm tempted to hold back and rest on my natural abilities, rather than allow God's abilities to express themselves through me. Wanting to dim or block the light within, to match the dimness of the environment around us, is like placing a bowl over a lamp (Matthew 5:15). We must be strong when the voices of shame speak. We must choose courage over comfort and cast off the bowl so others can see God's light shining in us. I pray that, in the face of shame, you will choose courage over comfort and let Christ's light shine without restraint. Doing so is your pathway to fulfillment.

~ The Nails and the Fence

There is an old story about a boy I'll call Zac who stayed on his grandparent's farm with his sister one summer. Zac's wise and loving grandfather became troubled as he heard his young charge saying mean and hurtful things to his little sister ... things like, "You are so ugly! No wonder you don't have friends!" The grandfather talked with his wife about the issue and they both prayed for a way to help their grandson understand the impact of his hurtful words.

That night, the grandfather awoke, inspired by an idea to teach Zac a lifelong lesson. A teachable moment arrived the next afternoon as Zac began tormenting his sister. "You're uglier and smellier than grandpa's pigs!" the boy sneered. The grandfather immediately called Zac over and handed him a jar of nails and a hammer. "Take a timeout in your room," the grandfather said. "But before you go, I want you to apologize to your sister and then hammer a nail into that old section of fence." From that point on, every time Zac said hurtful things, his grandfather enforced the same repercussion: an apology, a nail in the fence, and a timeout.

This disciplinary routine continued all summer until Zac's final day on the farm. As usual, the boy started in on his sister and Grandpa called him aside. Zac knew the routine. Only, this time, his grandfather changed the drill. "Look at that fence," he said. "How many nails do you think you've hammered in there?" The boy looked at the scarred fence and said in a somewhat sorrowful voice, "A hundred?" The grandpa handed Zac an empty jar and said, "Take the hammer and pull out every nail in the fence and count them in front of me."

Twenty minutes later, the boy returned and counted the nails. "Seventy-seven nails," Zac reported. Grandpa took the boy's little hand and led him back to the fence. "Look at this fence, son," he said. "It's just like your sister's heart. Every time you say something hurtful, you drive a nail into her heart."

Surprised by his grandpa's comment, tears started cascading down Zac's cheeks. "But Grandpa," he protested, "every time I said mean things, I apologized."

"Yes, you did," his grandfather replied. "But that is why I had you remove the nails from the fence. Your apology may have removed the nail, but look closely. There is still a hole that is left behind."

This is a perfect illustration of the pain many of us carry from other people's words and actions—wounds that have left our hearts filled with holes. How can we be fulfilled if our hearts have countless leaks? Many of us cannot even receive the blessing God desires to pour into us because we have so many gaping holes from negative experiences we have faced. We feel unworthy of God's blessings, or of having good things happen, or of becoming fulfilled. We begin to view our lives through the lens of our wounds and scars.

We all have scars from the wounds caused by others ... from the scratches and cuts of our childhood ... and from the long gashes left on our hearts by our adult experiences. Some scars are readily visible; others are invisible and remain hidden for fear of experiencing embarrassment or shame. In this life, there are countless inner wounds—griefs that never quite heal ... absolute wrongs that can never be righted ... memories that cannot be erased ... hurtful words and betrayals that all seem to have a mainline connection to pain and anguish. If not dealt with completely, these wounds, at best, may vanish for a season; but, eventually, like clockwork, they will return. For others, the wounds never vanish. They are present every moment of every day.

~ Our scars tell a story

Each scar we bear represents an event—a painful event. In John 20:20, Jesus appeared to his disciples with scars where the soldiers' nails and spear had pierced him. The disciples all examined the marks and, as they did, they believed in the story the scars told (The Gospel message)—the good news story of salvation forged from the wounds of Jesus Christ. Today, and for all eternity, Christ's scars are still telling salvation's story. Each painful flaw that left its mark on the flawless Christ tells of this familiar word: *s-a-l-v-a-t-i-o-n*. Sometimes, we become so familiar with things that, over time, they lose the attractiveness and shine they once had. I want you to reset your understanding of what salvation truly implies and its impact on you. I want to share a very powerful verse on salvation and break this down to gain better understanding.

"For I am not ashamed of the Gospel, for it is the power of God for salvation to everyone who believes" (Romans 1:16, ESV).

First, let's examine the word *gospel*. It is the story of the good news message of salvation through Jesus Christ. The Gospel is so much more than a story or a message in the context of our natural way of thinking. In fact, it's alive and active because it is God's Word (see Hebrews 4:12). John 1:14 says Jesus is the Word who became a person and lived among us. The Gospel is alive and active and is the embodiment of Jesus. So, we can see the Gospel is something that exists outside the realm of the natural. It is super-natural. Romans 1:16 also says the Gospel is "the power of God." This word "power" in the Greek is *dynamis*. It is where we get the word dynamite and dynamo in our English language. *Dynamis* is the explosive power or energy that produces miracles. In other words, it is the explosive power of God that produces miracles.

Now, let's come back to the word "salvation." Our Western doctrines, combined with our English Bible translations, have drastically diluted the meaning of salvation. In the Greek, salvation is *soteria* (used 46 times in the New Testament) and saved is *sozo* (used 110 times). The word's root meaning goes beyond just the forgiveness of sins. According to *Strong's Concordance*, salvation, from the Greek, is defined as "wholeness in body and spirit, being physically healed of diseases, and to be delivered from your enemy (the Devil and his demons)."

Salvation is more than the supreme gift of eternal life with God. He did not stop with the heavenly promise of salvation. He also gave us the earthly effects of it on our lives today! This salvation includes the benefits of being set free from demonic attacks and emotional oppression, and healing in our mind and physical body.

The story of the scars of Jesus Christ is the explosive supernatural power of salvation that brings about your total wholeness—spiritually, emotionally and physically. The scars tell the Gospel story of *your* deliverance from evil and past hurts. It tells the story of how your flaws are received and accepted and you are loved and forgiven—totally set free! The scars tell the story of your victory in Christ. The scars speak that Jesus knows what it's like to be pierced and carry your pain. His scars tell the story of triumphantly overcoming death on the cross. His scars tell the story that, even though he was nailed down, he did not stay down … *and neither shall you!* His scars tell the story of your scars, too … that you are not alone in your suffering and you, too, are an overcomer. The scars tell both of your story and Christ blended as one story of your salvation. He was pierced to bring about your fulfillment and release you from the wounds of the past.

Your vulnerabilities are the painful stories in your scars—vulnerabilities that must be touched by Christ.

Look at your scars (the stories and pain inside each one). Let him touch each one in his loving, comforting embrace. Let him heal you by the power of his salvation.

~ Prayer ~

Lord, I choose to partner with the power of Your salvation that is available for me. I exchange my wounds with what you chose to do for me on the cross. I trade all my past pains in exchange for Your exceeding joy. I trade my anxiety for Your peace. I receive Your love that replaces and drives out my fear.

Amen.

Mephibosheth — His Story and Mine

"Great sea captains are made in rough waters and deep seas."
~ Kathryn Kuhlman

I want to tell you my favorite story from the Bible. It's very personal to me and I've cherished it in my own little personal treasure chest as a reminder of how God sees me. But now, I believe God wants me to take it out, unpack it, and share it with you.

Mephibosheth is only mentioned in a few biblical passages, but his story reveals timeless truths and is endlessly inspiring. Let's start with the backstory. There are two Mephibosheths in the Bible. We will be studying the son of Jonathan, grandson of Israel's king, Saul.

If there ever were two people bound together as great friends, it was David and Jonathan. First Samuel 18:1 explains the relationship between Jonathan and

David this way: "After David had finished talking with Saul, Jonathan became one in spirit with David, and he loved him as himself." These words describe the tremendous bond between friends who'd fought wars, celebrated victories, and journeyed through many of life's up and downs together.

The main challenge to this relationship was Jonathan's father, who was jealous of David because God chose him to be Israel's king. All the people of the kingdom held David in high regard, even singing songs of his great victories in battle. Jealousy raged within King Saul so powerfully that he attempted to murder David. Even so, the bond of friendship between the Jonathan and David was never broken. Eventually, Jonathan married and had a family, including a son named Mephibosheth. Shortly after Mephibosheth's fifth birthday, Jonathan died in battle along with his father, King Saul. This triggered a chain of events that eventually led David to become the king, just as God had promised. It is here we begin Mephibosheth's story.

~ From the Mouth of Shame

Mephibosheth is first mentioned in Scripture in 2 Samuel 4:4 (NIV): "Jonathan son of Saul had a son who was lame in both feet. He was five years old when the news about Saul and Jonathan came from Jezreel. His nurse picked him up and fled, but as she hurried to leave, he fell and became disabled. His name was Mephibosheth."

Several important revelations are revealed in this one short passage. Notice the cause and effect within the text. It says Mephibosheth's nurse picked him up and fled but, as she hurried to leave, he fell (was dropped) and became disabled. Not only was he dropped, but he was dropped by someone on whom Mephibosheth depended upon—a trusted caregiver.

Like Mephibosheth, many of us have been dropped. In some cases, dropped by the people we trusted the most. Moms, dads, brothers, sisters, friends, teachers, lovers, and pastors, etc. It's one thing to drop yourself. But to be dropped by someone else is devastating, especially when you trusted, needed, or depended on the person who dropped you. This is an unforgettable, crippling experience for many of us. And it helps explain why so many are walking around today spiritually broken—limping through life because of past injuries.

Mephibosheth's name in Hebrew also reveals great insight on the nature of shame. You see, his name means, "from the mouth of shame." The definition of shame in the

Merriam-Webster's dictionary is:

1. The painful emotion caused by consciousness of guilt, shortcoming, or impropriety.

2. The condition of humiliating disgrace or disrepute.
3. Something that brings criticism, blame, something to be regretted.

Synonyms of shame are disgrace, embarrassment, humiliation, and dishonor. To reiterate the definition offered by Dr. Brené Brown, the world-renowned researcher on shame and vulnerability, shame is, "the intensely painful feeling or experience of believing that we are flawed and therefore unworthy of love and belonging—something we've experienced, done, or failed to do makes us unworthy of connection."

The "mouth of shame," described by Mephibosheth's name, reveals the strategy of the Enemy of Our Souls at work. The worldly culture spoke shame upon this boy and labeled him. Notice how the Scripture passage introduces him. He's not even called by his name. Instead, he's introduced as "a son who was lame in both feet." Isn't that just like the voice of shame? Think about it! **The mouth of shame will always speak of your disabilities but God will always speak of your abilities.**

We store these words that speak of our disabilities inside our spiritual backpack. When we agree with these negative, shaming words spoken into our lives— words like weak, slut, stupid, ugly, failure, unlovable, liar, thief, unwanted, crazy, and others—we create curses. Think about the negative agreements you've made in your mind about yourself. Each one of these agreements is a heavy stone in your pack.

The mouth of shame says YOU ARE the mistake. **There is a massive difference between the people who make mistakes versus the ones who say they ARE the mistake.** When we form agreements with these destructive voices, shame takes root, crippling you under the weight of its load. Shame grows and manifests in every part of your life, taking over your very personality as it tries to make you into its own image. It overgrows into all that you are—so much so, that it eventually intertwines with your subconscious and conscious mind, forming destructive actions and patterns. We begin to embody the very image of this toxic agreement—living it out and even passing it to those around us.

~ My Story from the Mouth of Shame

For me, the words that weighed me down and nearly destroyed me were "loser" and "stupid." Before we go any further, please understand: I have great parents of whom I'm very proud. They love the Lord and do their best to serve him. They are the most amazing, loving grandparents as well. I think my daughter would gladly trade a day with Grandma and Pop Pop to be with them any day of the week. They are overcomers in every sense of the word. So much so, that this book is dedicated to them. Their story is a testimony to the saving power of Jesus Christ that is available to anyone.

God has completely torn off the labels used to describe me in the past. To me, they truly are reminders of his miracle-working power. However, our family endured troubled times during my teen years. When I was between the ages of 14 and 18, my father began to sell drugs and it escalated to the point that it was his full-time job.

Back in those days, people saw my dad as tough and intimidating. But, to me, he was still my dad. I loved him and I knew he loved me. Even so, my life changed quickly during my teen years. I remember coming home from school one afternoon, grabbing a bowl of cereal, and sitting back on my couch to watch TV, only to find assault weapons under the couch cushions. That was my life back then. It was no movie. It was real.

Dad never talked about what he did for a living and did his best to hide it. But I knew exactly what was happening at that age and it affected me greatly. His crew would come by the house from time to time. They were always respectful to my mom, my brothers, and me. My dad was very careful to allow only a few people to visit our home. I knew some of these people were very dangerous but, to me, they had become almost like part of our family. I knew the two hiding spots where my dad stored his cash. It was always neatly stacked in the rafters of our garage or above the light fixture in our bathroom. Drugs were never around in plain sight; my dad always made sure of that.

After a couple years, I noticed things changing. I began overhearing conversations about people tailing our family's Suburban as we made our way through town. Police raided our home numerous times over the course of a few years. Each time, they would leave empty-handed with no evidence.

We lived in the same, decent, home in the Los Angeles suburbs my entire childhood until I was eighteen. I knew my neighbors well and had many friends. In the summertime, in the years before the drug business started, we'd play games all day outside. However, those relationships were all destroyed as police began to interview our neighbors. Seeing a battering ram knocking down our front door as the DEA and LAPD raided our home marked our family as damaged and dangerous.

I lost all my friends. Nobody would let their children be friends with the dangerous drug dealer's son. I would hear other kids say I was a loser. I had a hard enough time with school even before these things started happening. But, now, everything at school started to crumble around me.

The girl I was dating said our school counselor had called her in and told her that I was a loser and would never amount to anything. Many teachers formed opinions of me without truly knowing me. I was always on the lookout because of a group of guys from school who'd hunt me down and try to jump me.

You see, I was dropped by someone I trusted and I began to make agreements within myself, based on the words others had spoken into my life. The opinions people had of me took hold and I began to believe and agree that I was the stupid loser and troublemaker that they said I was. I made agreements with myself that I was not worthy of friendship or acceptance.

Rejection became my identity and I hated all authority in my life because of that rejection. Eventually, I even began to ruin the good relationships in my life because of my ironclad belief that I was not good enough to be truly loved and accepted. I felt I had to pretend to be someone else in order to fit in and be loved. Unfortunately, my coping technique of holding family secrets and living a fake life back-fired. Achieving intimacy became impossible because everything about my authentic self was hidden and locked up tight.

I destroyed some good relationships over those years. I had become the troublemaker—and, eventually, the lawbreaker—everyone said I would be. My early twenties were even more difficult. Sure, someone dropped me as a kid. But, now, as a young adult, I began habitually dropping myself ... so many times, in fact, that brokenness became my normal. I learned to hide it well, wearing a mask that everything was OK. I would telegraph confidence to the world, but it was so over-inflated it came off as arrogant.

When the mouth of shame speaks its lies, we respond in two ways: we shrink back or puff up. I became puffed up. Everything I did was always exaggerated to make me appear bigger than everyone else, in an effort to compensate for the smallness I truly felt inside. As time passed, anything and everything triggered this root of rejection inside of me. I believed I was unworthy of love and felt I had to be someone else to earn love. I would lash out before anyone could possibly get close enough to hurt me again. This became the cycle of my adult life. I'll share more of my story in later pages but, for now, let's revisit the story of Mephibosheth.

~ Prayer ~

Lord, I pray that the mouth of shame be forced shut in my life. I pray You mute shame's voices and open myself to hear only Your voice instead. Lord, please allow me to hear of my capabilities and my acceptance through Jesus Christ. I willingly choose to live believing the truth of Your word and reject those voices of shame. Today I declare no to shame and yes to Christ!

Amen.

~ Shame Breaker 7 ~

Disrupt the Vortex of Gossip

*"What you don't see with your eyes,
don't witness with your mouth."*
~ Jewish Proverb

Years have gone by and now Mephibosheth is a man. Second Samuel 9:1-13 begins to explain the unfolding events. David (who is now Israel's king) desires to find any living family members of his dear friend Jonathan (who is now dead). David wants to show kindness to his best friend's descendants.

In 2 Samuel 9:1-5 (NIV), we read:

"David asked, 'Is there anyone still left of the house of Saul to whom I can show kindness for Jonathan's sake?'

Now there was a servant of Saul's household named Ziba. They summoned him to appear before David, and the king said to him, 'Are you Ziba?'

'At your service,' he replied.

The king asked, 'Is there no one still alive from the house of Saul to whom I can show God's kindness?'

Ziba answered the king, 'There is still a son of Jonathan; he is lame in both feet.'

'Where is he?' the king asked.

Ziba answered, 'He is at the house of Makir son of Ammiel in Lo Debar.'

So King David had him brought from Lo Debar, from the house of Makir son of Ammiel."

Notice, in verse 3, the king asked, "Is there no one still alive from the house of Saul to whom I can show God's kindness?" Ziba answered the king, "There is still a son of Jonathan; he is lame in both feet." Significantly, Ziba doesn't tell David Mephibosheth's name. Instead, Ziba calls the boy by his disability: "Jonathan's son, he is lame in both feet." Consequently, Ziba formed an agreement and partnered with what came from the mouth of shame. In many ways sometimes we become the voice shame speaks through when we partner with its saying.

I don't think Ziba intended to label Mephibosheth in a negative light; it was just the word on the street. In the same way, many good people can execute judgment, bringing shame from careless words and attitudes.

In today's culture, it's so easy to be swept up in the vortex of all the chattering voices of shame aimed at our lives. Notice, for example, how social media is shame-driven to its core. We can become so desensitized and conditioned by pervasive shame messages that we forget the electronic boulders being thrown are damaging real, live human beings.

Shame-inducing gossip is pervasive and as old as civilization, itself. Like gravity, gossip has an uncanny ability to pull everything within its reach into its nightmarish vortex. Take the workplace, for example. Let's say you've been promoted into a new department. Over the past year, you've been working hard to win this position and praying earnestly about working with this new team. On the first day in your new position, you run into someone who used to work in your department. They inform you that your new boss, John, is a lazy jerk who never does anything but bark orders all day. And, oh, by the way, he's an alcoholic.

A seed—a word containing someone else's opinions, theories, and beliefs—has just been deposited into the soil of your mind. However, you're not aware of the seed-sower's motivation for telling you these details. They could be angry about not being adequate for the job or they might be making an assumption based on someone else's seeds of fear and judgment. But, because you've let the seed take root in your mind, some part of you believes the gossip.

You enter your workspace and meet your new boss. As he speaks, you feel a poisonous weed spring up inside you, but you don't realize you're viewing your new boss through the eyes of the co-worker who shared this gossip. Before long, you begin gossiping to co-workers, tossing out your own seeds about the boss. And, one by one, others start perceiving the boss through your lens. After a while, you really dislike your new position and conclude that you're in a dead-end job. You blame the boss; but, in reality, the toxic seeds of gossip choking your soul are to blame for your unfulfillment.

Gossip will always try to typecast who you are in society. At various times, we all play the role of victim and perpetrator. The world is trapped in an identity crisis characterized by people wearing the wrong labels. No wonder so many people feel unfulfilled and shamed within this worldly culture. When we gossip, we are partnering with dark forces in the spirit realm, whose main focus is to steal, kill, and destroy the fulfillment of everything God offers us.

Now, imagine this behavior continuing in an endless web of connection between all humanity in our world. The consequence is a defiling, contagious illness with symptoms that manifest as all things destructive, driven by fear and shame. It produces the mind of this worldly culture, the mind of our destroyer. We see in the 2 Samuel 9: 1-5 passage that Ziba was participating in the community's gossip and, by doing so, he was partnering with the mouth of shame. He was actually the mouthpiece the voice of shame spoke through. When we speak about others in a way that equates their worth with their disability, we are partnering with this world's evil forces, which desire to bring hell on earth. God desires to build his kingdom within us and that starts with defining who we are in Christ. When you gossip about others, with whom are you choosing to partner? Is it our Enemy, whose goal is "on earth as it is in hell?" Or, is it our loving Heavenly Father whose goal is "on earth as it is in heaven?" Are you partnering with blessing or cursing? Life or death? I pray you commit to continually choose God's side and speak his life into others around you.

~ Prayer ~

Lord, I choose to partner with blessing and speak Your language of love and truth. Heal me from the wounds of gossip that have impacted my life. Forgive me for partnering with the voice of shame and speaking gossip about others. I ask that the pull of You, Holy Spirit, is stronger than the vortex of gossip. Use me to be a force of encouragement, releasing the power of Your word to those around me.

Amen.

Cancel the Lo Debar State of Mind

"God never takes away something from your life without replacing it with something better."
~ Billy Graham

Let's revisit the verses that first mention Mephibosheth's whereabouts. "And the king said unto him, 'Where is he?' And Ziba said unto the king, 'Behold, he is in the house of Makir, the son of Ammiel, in Lo Debar.' So King David had him brought from Lo Debar, from the house of Makir son of Ammiel" (2 Samuel 9:4-5, NIV).

Notice the name of the town where Mephibosheth lives: Lo Debar. In Hebrew, the name is translated as a place with no pasture, meaning a place of no provision … a place of nothing. However, the meaning goes much deeper than that. *Deba*r normally means "word" or "thing." The prefix *lo* is a negator; thus, the term *Lo Debar* means "no word" or "no thing." So, basically, Mephibosheth was living in a state of nothingness. No words of encouragement. No hope for a future. He was living in a constant state of abject lack.

When we make agreements with the mouth of shame that speaks out against us, our lives can begin to reflect a Lo Debar effect. Subconsciously, we begin choosing a life cursed with nothingness. It is a state of mind that forms an agreement that declares, "I am nothing and I deserve nothing." It is a life of complete unfulfillment. We build a house on it and call it home; but our house, in reality, is shame's jail cell. This is where our dear brother, Mephibosheth, is living.

Do you feel, to some degree, like you're living there, too? Don't lose hope. This story and your story are not finished. God has a plan!

My own personal Lo Debar was marked by painful isolation resulting from years of not feeling good enough. I disguised my authentic self in a desperate attempt to prove I was tough and that I didn't need love. But the truth was I craved it continually. It's interesting how **the very thing we desire most is sometimes the thing we push away with the most force.** Isn't that how this worldly culture trains us?

The desire to hide in Lo Debar can be so powerful. We run into its shelter of secrecy, silence, and judgment because of the unworthiness we feel deep down. If you can muster the courage to accept the king's invitation, walk out of your Lo Debar prison cell, and earnestly seek your personal freedom, you will discover that it's only a matter of time before you find what you are looking for. God does not want you to hate yourself and live in a self-imposed prison. He desires to give you good things because he loves you and knows your value. You are worth so much more than a life trapped in Lo Debar. Jesus paid the ultimate price—his life—for your freedom! So, love yourself, respect yourself, and honor yourself because God does the same toward you. I promise that before the end of this book you will be well on your way of living in freedom. He is calling you out of Lo Debar because you are worth it!

~ Prayer ~

King Jesus, please help me to walk out from the jail cell of lack and regret and bring me into your presence. I leave behind the old life of Lo Debar and choose to welcome the adventure of your invitation. I choose to say yes to what you have for my future even if I don't understand it yet. I cast off all fear that holds me in Lo Debar and embrace your call to come.

Amen.

~ Shame Breaker 9 ~

Receive Grace in God's Greeting

"Do not think your temporary setback is outside of the power of Jesus' permanent comeback."
~ Benny Perez

"When Mephibosheth son of Jonathan, the son of Saul, came to David, he bowed down to pay him honor. David said, 'Mephibosheth.' 'At your service,' he replied" (2 Samuel 9:6, NIV).

This short, simple passage displays the greeting between the two men. Notice how David responded to Mephibosheth. He called him by his name. He did not call him by the labels the world gave him. Remember how the servant, Ziba, identified Mephibosheth as "the cripple, lame in both feet." As you continue in this book you will notice a theme. **Shame will always call you by your disability, but God will always call you by your abilities and blessings.**

David reflects the character of God in this passage. I believe God looked at Mephibosheth and saw an overcomer. Yes, his name might mean "from the mouth of shame," but God saw a man who would overcome that mouth ... and even shut it!

Grace was the first greeting Mephibosheth encountered from the king. It is the perfect illustration of God's grace towards us. But what is grace? In Christian circles, we toss this word around a lot. First, let us look at what it is not. Grace is not obtained by accomplishments or success. In fact, God's grace is not earned in any way at all. It cannot be purchased. No education, occupation, or fame can obtain it! You can't earn it by memorizing the whole Bible or praying 8 hours a day. Rather, it is the unmerited favor of God that is given as a free gift. You and I are accepted, and expected to walk in God's unmerited favor.

Author James L. Gordon most eloquently wrote, "Kindness is the green grass near the hard pebbles of the road." In the same way, God's grace is His loving-kindness laid before us. The road of life might be long and rough under foot, but God's grace somehow makes the journey softer, like plush, green grass. The road you tread might be uneasy and painful, but God's grace is right there if you are willing, by faith, to step onto it. Ironically, the awareness of being unqualified to walk in God's grace is the actual entryway. All are welcome to walk this path. Simply take a step of faith and let grace be the solid ground under your feet, safely supporting you.

The next passage illustrates four specific manifestations of God's amazing grace. We see them as the king announces his intentions to bring his grace (unmerited favor) upon Mephibosheth. He tells the broken man from Lo Debar the following:

"'Don't be afraid,' David said to him, 'for I will surely show you kindness for the sake of your father Jonathan. I will restore to you all the land that belonged to your grandfather Saul, and you will always eat at my table'" (2 Samuel 9:7, NIV).

God's grace toward us is always transformational, touching our lives in these four special ways. In the next four chapters, we'll lean into these four key embodiments of God's amazing grace.

1. Don't be afraid.
2. I will surely show you kindness.
3. I will restore to you.
4. You will always eat at my table.

~ Prayer ~

Lord Jesus, I ask for wisdom and revelation to know the grace you have for me. As I read further, please open my eyes to see and mind to understand the vast power and blessing Your grace provides for my life.

Amen.

~ Shame Breaker 10 ~

"Do Not Be Afraid"

*"First we must unflinchingly face our fears
and honestly ask ourselves why we are afraid."*
~ Martin Luther King Jr.

L et me ask you something. What is your relationship with fear? We all have a relationship with it.
For some of us, it's like a distant relative that pops in
on momentous occasions. Or, fear can be like an
abusive spouse with whom you live daily. No matter
what type of relationship you have with it, fear is part
of the human condition. It's the alarm system that
screams for us to run away from danger, fight to
protect ourselves, or freeze in hopes that the danger
will pass us by, unharmed.

The problem is, sometimes our internal "fear alarm"
goes off when there is no actual threat. It is a false alarm,
a false fire that can lead us into a life of distraction
and turmoil, and lead us away from our personal fulfillment. It torments us into living in continuous agony,
a Lo Debar state of hell on earth. Instead of encouraging
us to expose our vulnerabilities so we can receive help

and healing, fear keeps us searching for ways to protect ourselves. It destroys the ability to trust the trustworthy people and situations around us. This occurs because we see the world through the eyes of past pain.

Imagine that your thoughts are like your own hand. You can touch things with your healthy hands. You can build things with them, feed yourself, and even use them to hold and love others. Your hands are also made for awareness and the sensation of feeling by touching. Without them, you'd drop everything you try to hold. Now, imagine your hands are injured. They've been cut and infected. If you touch the infected hand, it's painful. So you try to protect your hand. With this priority, you cannot enjoy building things, feeding yourself, or holding others in love because being touched is painful.

Now, imagine that every person has this hand infection. Nobody can touch anyone, build with anyone, or feed anyone else because it's too painful.

Our wonderful minds can become exactly like this description of an infected hand. We all have some degree of infection resulting from the emotional wounds that have been inflicted on us. As in the case of Mephibosheth, the result of being dropped has opened a wound. Our wound, however, is invisible … it's in our mind. And we react with fear, keeping everyone away.

I'm reminded of a time we lived in the country. I told my daughter that the deck had splinters and that, if she went outside, she'd need to wear shoes. Despite my warning, she went outside without shoes and got a splinter in her foot. Fearing punishment, she hid from my wife and me the fact that she'd gotten a splinter. A week went by before I noticed she was limping.

I asked to look at my daughter's foot and saw it was infected. She confessed that she hadn't sought help because she didn't want to be punished or have us think she was bad. Even now, fearing the pain, she was reluctant to let me get close to her inflamed foot. I told her I could remove the source of the pain but, to do so, she'd need to trust me and give me access. I said it would hurt a bit but, after a few moments, the pain would be over and healing could begin. Finally, she conceded and allowed me to gently extract the splinter that had caused her so much discomfort. And, sure enough, her foot was soon completely healed.

In the same way, we all have emotional splinters that we try and hide and ignore. The problem is, over time, our efforts can cripple our walk. Which explains why so many of us lumber through life with a spiritual limp. We hide our wounds and protect them. But is our protection actually helpful? No! In reality, we're inviting infection to set in. And, once infection takes up residence within our pain, it begins to spread its poison to other parts of the body.

We cannot always control what happens in our lives. Life isn't always fair and we can't always get everything that we want. Brother Mephibosheth's life perfectly illustrates these truths. The most important thing we need to realize is that **we are *always* in complete control over the way we handle every situation that is thrown our way.** We must learn how to "train that brain," as my wife, the therapist, always says. We do this by focusing on the things that we *do* have power over and finding the courage to let go of situations that didn't work out as we'd hoped. Take the opportunity to partner with God's plan to transform your life. Allow God and others to get close enough to help you remove your splinters.

Sometimes we've lived with our toxic agreements for so long they've become like prison walls. Change often is intimidating because we don't know what lies ahead. The very thought of leaving a familiar environment, even a harmful one, can be very frightening. The term is called *institutionalized.* Many long-term inmates report that the fear of life outside their familiar prison bars—the institution—is greater than the desire to be free.

The untruthful agreements we've made with ourselves are holding many of us back. Until we choose to overcome our fear and break these agreements, we're likely to remain spiritually and emotionally stuck, never reaching the full potential—or enjoying the fulfillment—God has for our lives ... wonderful plans such as those described in Jeremiah 29:11, NIV: "'For I know the plans I have for you,' declares the LORD, 'plans to prosper you and not to harm you, plans to give you hope and a future.'"

Please receive this: God's heart is FOR you NOT against you. A fulfilled life is a life that is constantly evolving and transforming. Fulfillment is being able to handle what life throws your way, using your mental capacity to build on both the good and the bad that life brings, and using it all to your advantage.

Speaking from experience, and based on God's Word, I know that handling life's curve balls can only be done through the Holy Spirit living in us. God's Spirit teaches us the importance of learning to embrace change with open arms rather than fear. We must reach the place of understanding that God is good even when we don't understand life's pain and heartache. We must see ourselves through God's eyes, realizing that God is total love and it's alright to be flawed. That is what the cross is for. It's the ultimate love story—a true story—and you are the main object of His affection.

Religion filtered through the culture of this world has defiled this truth and has attempted to turn our heads away from it, just as I turned my opponent's head in that martial arts match decades ago. We get so hung up on not feeling good enough to be loved that we push away the very thing we need most—love and community—fearing we'll be rejected. We fear we will be figured out … that our flaws (our splinters) will be found.

Embed this deeply in your mind and heart: It's your flaws that make you wonderful and only love can extract the fear from your flaws and remove the shame you carry. Just as David said to Mephibosheth, "Do not be afraid," Jesus the King is saying to you, "Do not be afraid." Like Mephibosheth, your flaws and vulnerabilities make you unique. They underscore your unique love story, which is all-the-more wonderful because you are embraced unconditionally, even with your imperfections. Scripture reminds us, "There is no fear in love. But perfect love drives out fear because fear has to do with punishment. The one who fears is not made perfect in love" (1 John 4:18). I would add that love not only drives out fear but it also perfects our flawed selves in God's sight, removing every excuse for shame. Nothing else in all creation has the power to do this—only the love of God.

~Prayer ~

I realize You know every struggle in my daily life. The person I am, and the person the world wants me to be. Calm my thoughts and emotions and open my heart to your peace, comfort, and wisdom. Help me not to live in fear of rejection for who I am. Please reduce the feelings of fear and anxiety that plague me. Help me rest in You and trust in your love. As I navigate through this broken world let your love be my compass. Let your love be my certainty that leads me to the Fulfillment you have for me. In Your name I pray, Jesus.

Amen.

Love Courageously "I Will Surely Show You Kindness"

"With the same intensity that the Father loves Jesus, He loves you."
~ Mike Bickle

Before we continue, it's important to understand that God's love is full of power. It is supernatural and it destroys Satan's strongholds like nothing else. God's love does not fear, but, instead, kicks fear out. His love is not intimidated by evil. All sin, evil, wickedness, traumas, and mistakes place heavy chains of shame and fear on you. But there is no shackle that God's love cannot break.

I remember one Sunday morning, as I walked into church, three board members approached me. "A man in one of the classrooms talks in a different voice and hisses like a cat each time we begin to pray for him," they said. This would not be my first time to confront a situation like this. Each instance is different and I always learn a lesson from every encounter.

As I entered the room, a man I'll call Jim was sitting in a chair. About 30 years old, he was sweating and looked afraid. Immediately, I was overcome by tremendous love for this man. I recognized his torment and knew right away that God was showing me his great love for this beleaguered soul. The love I felt was beyond words, but I will do my best to explain it.

You see, God's love is also God's truth. You cannot separate love and truth when they come from God. They are comingled together as one mighty force. As we began our encounter, I gently shared what God was revealing regarding his love for Jim. Then I prayed that God's arrow of love and truth would penetrate deep within him. Sure enough, as I prayed, God's precise truth, like an arrow, powerfully pierced this young man's heart. His body contorted as his spine curved upward, cat-like, and he began to hiss at me. At that point, I noticed a protective feeling of relaxed authority enveloping me as I said, "In the name of Jesus, get out of God's child." Immediately, Jim's face changed as he began to weep, thanking and praising God. His body was relaxed and he was full of peace. God's love was thick in that room and we stayed for a while just soaking in and praising God for His love.

Jim began to share how he had done things that he could never forgive himself for and he was always tormented by fear and shame. But, as he experienced God's love, the chains of Jim's deep-seated fear were broken and he was free. He began to allow the Holy Spirit to remove the splinters of his sinful choices and healing began.

About 3 years later, I ran into Jim and he excitedly shared how free he was and how God had led him, through a deep spiritual and emotional healing process, to break his ties to depression and unforgiveness. He had a family and a good job, and was part of a great church in his community.

I don't share this story to evoke fear that the Devil is under every rock. But it's important to remember that he exists and he is roaming the earth, seeking to devour whom he may (1 Peter 5:8). Thankfully, God is ready, willing, and able to set free, through his loving truth, all who come to him. Sometimes, however, it's not the Enemy at all who torments and traps us. In fact, most times, we are our own worst enemy. Though we often sabotage ourselves, when we call on the Lord, he will lovingly begin the inner healing work, through the Holy Spirit, to deal with our issues. No matter the situation, the remedy is always the same: lovingkindness. Love your God, love yourself, and love others (Matthew 12:30-31). That is the essence of being a Shame Breaker and Fulfillment Maker.

As we continue to learn more about King David and Mephibosheth, we see God's lovingkindness unfold. You'll recall David telling his dear friend's son, "I will surely show you kindness for the sake of your father Johnathan." The word used here for "kindness" is most often translated "lovingkindness." Notice David didn't say "because you are flawless or perfect, I will show you kindness." Rather, David chose to extend his love and kindness to Mephibosheth because he was Jonathan's descendant. Just as Jonathan earned the right for the king's blessing to be passed down to Jonathan's children, Jesus earned the right for us to receive the blessing and favor of Father God.

Jesus' heart's cry for us is beautifully explained in John 17:20-25 (NIV) which is the Savior's prayer for believers throughout the ages:

"I am not asking on behalf of them alone (the disciples), but also on behalf of those who will believe in Me through their message, that all of them may be one, as You, Father, are in Me, and I am in You. May they also be in Us, so that the world may believe that You sent Me. I have given them the glory You gave Me, so that they may be one as We are one—I in them and You in Me—that they may be perfectly united, so that the world may know that You sent Me and have loved them just as You have loved Me."

Consider the significance of Jesus' words in verse 23, "…[you] have loved them even as You have loved me." What a powerful statement! God the Father of our Lord Jesus Christ loves you with the same intensity and dedication as he loves Christ. You are united and completely comingled with Christ Jesus and God the Father. Many of you will have difficulty receiving this. For generations, religious traditions have spoken through the mouth of shame, creating division rather than unity in spirit. Look again at John 17 (Berean Study Bible). This time, focus on verse 26, "I have made Your name known to them and will continue to make it known, so that the love You have for Me may be in them, and I in them."

Jesus said it again in this passage, "… so that the love You have for Me may be in them, and I in them." God's love and kindness free us from shame and lead us into fulfillment in Christ. Pray along with me for the revelation of knowing the love God personally holds for you:

~ **Prayer** ~

Heavenly Father, in Jesus' name, I break all lies over my life. I break all false beliefs and agreements I hold within myself that you do not love me, unlike your word declares. I receive your truth—that the same love that you, Father God, have for Jesus, is also fully available to me. I receive that I am accepted and I am loved because of the bond between you, your Son, Jesus, and me. Thank you, Lord!

Amen.

~ Fulfillment Taker 2 ~

The Project Called Self
"I Will Restore to You"

*"We delight in the beauty of the butterfly,
but rarely admit the changes it has gone
through to achieve that beauty."*
~ Maya Angelou

"I will restore to you all the land that belonged to your grandfather Saul." (2 Samuel 9:7)

The word "restore" means "to bring back what was lost … to refresh and repair." Have you ever watched all the steps involved in restoration? Turn on the TV nowadays and you can't avoid it. Home renovations shows, with the big reveal at the end, abound. My wife and I sometimes are amazed at the before-and-after pictures as broken, ugly houses are masterfully transformed into homes of beauty and value.

The restoration process is never fast and easy. Before a magnificent new home can be revealed, the house is often torn down to the bare structure—

through a costly, lengthy, messy process—in order to rebuild it into something infinitely more wonderful than before. I used to work with a general contractor and every job got messy. It would be so nice if God's restoration process were as easy as slapping on a fresh coat of paint. But many sequential steps are involved and no single step can be skipped, or the process will remain incomplete.

Let's examine the steps of restoration. Consider your mind, your will, your emotions, and even your body, as a home because that is exactly what they are. You live inside yourself. Houses will come and go. Apartments will come and go. But you are your own home. You're always there. You have the freedom to decorate it any color you want. You can choose to make essential repairs and do upkeep. Some of us have neglected our home for so long that we need a professional to come in and demolish certain areas that years of neglect have caused to decay and rot. It's time to allow the Carpenter of Nazareth, Jesus Christ, to come into your internal home and do his best work. Allow him to walk every room, every closet. Allow him to open the blueprints of the kingdom of heaven that he desires to build in you.

This kingdom is for you and your fulfillment is contained within it. He will ask you to toss some things out and you may not have the strength to do it, but he will do the heavy lifting. He will be your strength. As you begin your journey to silence the voice of shame and unleash your identity in Christ, will you invite the Carpenter of Nazareth inside? Some of you asked him to start the remodeling project called "self," but chose to pause the construction. Let him back in. Give him permission to complete the process. It's time to become a Shame Breaker and Fulfillment Maker!

~ Demolition Brings Desperation

The first thing you do in any restoration process is get rid of everything that doesn't add value—things that are outdated, unsightly, or unsound. Just like sanding down a hardwood floor, God must strip away everything that doesn't conform to the character of Christ, which is his ultimate goal for each of us (Romans 8:29). He must remove every independent, ego-driven part of us that believes, "I've got this! I don't need God." Sometimes the restoration process is painful and slow, but God is a master craftsman, the carpenter from Nazareth. He knows how to safely smooth the rough edges of our souls.

He also understands that each project is different. There's no such thing as a one-size-fits-all restoration. Some jobs require more demolition than others. Comparisons can derail God's work in your life. I can't compare my restoration project to my neighbor's because I don't know what's going on underneath my neighbor's baseboards, so to speak. Only the Nazarene carpenter, Jesus Christ, knows. Trust God's demolition process.

I suspect that Mephibosheth's demolition was the only way God's blessing and testimony of kindness could be fully revealed. **Without the test, there can be no testimony.** Remember Mephibosheth's grandfather was King Saul. He had land and titles and all the great wealth that the Philistines eventually plundered from his family. There was no inheritance for Mephibosheth. He was from Lo Debar. He owned nothing. Lack was his daily ration. He even lived in someone else's home.

Have you ever experienced a similar situation in your life when, one day, everything was demolished? Have you ever grasped at anything that could pull you out of your shocking situation? Sometimes the demolition stage slays our ego, bringing us to a place where we recognize how desperately we need God. Looking at Mephibosheth's story, even the proud family of a king is brought to its knees when demolition comes. You cannot be desperate for God when you are proud.

In so many ways, I can see this age-old battle within the church. Elitism and ego always block the desperation required for God's people to reach their full potential. Our revelation of how much we need

God determines the fulfillment of the church reaching the world with power and effectiveness.

As I write this, the world is besieged by the COVID-19 pandemic and the United States is being ravaged by riots, wildfires, hurricanes, political turmoil, and a debt-laden economy. It's a perfect example of demolition generating desperation. The Bible section at a Walmart was recently completely sold out. Only empty book racks could be seen. When our hearts are right, demolition truly does bring desperation for God and that is the perfect climate for revival.

~ Your Blueprints Must Have God's Fingerprints

The blueprints to your fulfillment are carefully drafted by God. Psalm 139:14-16 (TPT) perfectly illustrates his divine plan.

> "I thank you, God, for making me so mysteriously complex!
> Everything you do is marvelously breathtaking.
> It simply amazes me to think about it!
> How thoroughly you know me, Lord!
> You even formed every bone in my body
> when you created me in the secret place,
> carefully, skillfully shaping me from nothing
> to something.

You saw who you created me to be before
I became me!
Before I'd ever seen the light of day,
the number of days you planned for me
were already recorded in your book."

God already knows what the full potential of your life will look like. It was already pre-planned. However, through your free will, you have the prerogative to choose your own plans. You can take the pen from the architect of your life and draw your own blueprints for fulfillment.

When I work at jobsites with contractors, there's always a designated place where the project blueprints are laid out. Contractors continually put their fingers on the drawings to form strategies and identify next steps. The paper plans are full of fingerprints from the hands that carefully examine them while doing the work. Likewise, the plans for our lives should have both our fingerprints and God's all over them. It is a partnership that rests on God's planning and that requires our trust and cooperation.

Planning and rebuilding is a difficult stage in the restoration process. We don't often get to see God's plans unrolled and visible in their entirety. This can test our faith but, even in these times, we can be sure His process is at work within us. We touch God's plans with our hands of faith and begin to partner with him as the framing goes up. Then, as each step is completed, the next step unfolds in the process until the project is complete. Over time, we begin to see God's restoration project unfolding, and His plans are always building something good within us. "He has made everything beautiful in its time" (Ecclesiastes 3:11, WEB).

I strongly suspect that Brother Mephibosheth believed the only plan for his life was the demolition phase. Have you ever felt that way? You cry out, "Is this ever going to end?" Remember, God never leaves the work incomplete. He always finishes what he starts (Philippians 1:6). Our responsibility is to keep giving him permission to stay on the job site and let him complete his work.

~ The Revealing

In the physical realm, once a structure is remodeled, you recognize something new has been formed. This is where the fun begins. Color and decorations are added and the result is stunning. The tumultuous season is over and you have a beautifully restored masterpiece.

God does the same thing in our lives! Once the heavy demolition and rebuilding is complete, He fills us with joy and peace and blesses us with good things to the point where we could never imagine settling for the life we knew before. We become whole, complete, and beautiful. That's what God's fulfillment accomplishes as it's revealed in our lives. This reveal displays the greatness of God at work in our lives. It also demonstrates that we have overcome by the power of Christ within us (Col 1:27). Our transformation will always reveal God's habitation. It is the story of beauty from ashes.

"... to all who mourn in Israel, he will give a crown of beauty for ashes, a joyous blessing instead of mourning, festive praise instead of despair. In their righteousness, they will be like great oaks that the LORD has planted for his own glory (Isaiah 61:3, NLT).

Restoration is not an easy process. But when we choose to trust God through what might feel like a protracted, messy ordeal, he promises to transform our broken, hurting places into something truly amazing.

~ Prayer ~

Lord Jesus, help me to surrender to Your process of restoration. I know You are the Carpenter of Nazareth and by Your capable hands I am made perfect. Clear out every part of myself that is not productive and build Your kingdom within me. Give me the strength to obey when I am weak and help me to stand when I have fallen. I choose to roll up my sleeves and join you in creating the fulfilling life you have planned for me. I say YES to Your restoration in my life!

Amen.

Power of Belonging "You Will Always Eat at My Table"

"Those who have a strong sense of love and belonging have the courage to be imperfect."
~Brené Brown

Tables are one of the most central places of human connection. We are often fully alive to life when sharing a meal around a table. It's no surprise, then, to see this ritual displayed throughout the Bible. God has a way of showing up at tables. In fact, it's worth noting that, at the center of the spiritual lives of God's people in both the Old and New Testaments, we find a table: the table of Passover and the table of Communion. And when Jesus, himself, wanted to explain to his disciples what his impending death and new covenant was all about, he didn't give them a philosophy lesson, he gave them a seat at his table, and then gave them a meal.

I remember one year when I was a teen, not having a place to celebrate Thanksgiving. My home at the time was broken and I had nowhere to go. I remember the feeling of loneliness, seeing all the families preparing to gather for the traditional American holiday, remembering the times when my whole family would celebrate together. I was dating a girl at the time and her parents found out about my troubled family life. They had such compassion for me that they invited me to stay with them for the holiday and share Thanksgiving dinner. They did everything in their ability to make me feel like a family member that day.

How wonderful it was to feel accepted just as I was—a flawed, broken kid from the wrong side of the tracks. I didn't have to pretend to be perfect or act as if my family's situation was normal. I admit, at first it was uncomfortable. After all, I was revealing my vulnerability to these people. Not all of my vulner-abilities—no, not by a longshot, but at least some of them. The feeling was liberating even though I allowed only a little portion of my pain and weakness to be exposed. The smiles and the laughing and conver-sation felt totally freeing to me. I forgot for that moment that I'd been dropped by someone I trusted. In that moment, I belonged to this family. They'd provided their fellowship.

Most of us have struggled our whole lives with belonging. Something is always whispering, "If I can be part of something bigger than myself, I'll be fulfilled." This longing to belong is buried deep within our subconsciousness. The longing to belong can be a healthy, God-given desire, or it can be a trap if we feel we don't belong. It can be used as the antidote to bring healing from the places shame has touched, or it can deal a crippling blow when used incorrectly.

To have fulfilling relationships, you need the "longing to belong" part of you made healthy. In many ways, this aspect of your soul determines the fruitfulness of your life. But shame always pushes against you. If not resisted, it can cause you to slip into isolation and separation, forming agreements that true belonging is merely a pipedream. The isolation and separation, over time, bring loneliness—one of the poisonous fruits of shame. You see, **wherever love and belonging are absent, suffering flourishes.** As with Mephibosheth, it always speaks of your disabilities. In fact, is says "you do not belong."

In Chapter 11, we examined the fight, flight, or freeze responses that often characterize our reaction to suffering as well as our relationship with fear. Now, let's examine in more depth how fear affects our sense of belonging when shame speaks. We can run and hide from the world, forming no relationships with others. Or, we can build a thick wall, keeping others out and, at the same time, keeping ourselves locked inside. The second strategy describes a prison. Nobody comes in and nobody goes out. We are locked up, tight and afraid. This depicts the flight response to the fear of being rejected for who we truly are.

Next is the fight response. I have recognized this tendency within myself over the years as my knee-jerk response to shame. The fight is for the purpose of belonging. In fact, I think many of us fall into this category. The desire to belong is so great that we'll compromise who we are to fit into whatever group we feel will bring about our fulfillment.

Remember the labels I spoke about in previous chapters? In the case of trying to belong, we don't struggle with labels the world gives us but, rather, with labels we create for ourselves. Our self-styled labels are seamlessly connected to the fear of not belonging. To fit into someone or something else's community, we bedazzle our labels using metaphorical sequins, beads, glitter, lights, and rhinestones, hiding the precious gems inside.

Our culture has created a society that exchanges authentic jewels for fake ones. In the same way, we also exchange the real light for fake light. We cover the pain and wounds inflicted by life's pressures. But if nature has taught us anything, it's that time spent under pressure produces priceless diamonds and creates enduring worth. We would not be who we are without spending time under pressure letting God's light shine off our beautiful gemstone edges.

The worldly culture's view has manipulated many of us into discounting and failing to perceive our worth in hopes of belonging to something. We attribute no value to things that are the most valuable, fighting furiously, instead, to keep our labels from being torn off. What a travesty to pay such a high price in the pressures of this life and not use them to celebrate your worth and the worth of others.

Every part of our society—including government, religion, technology, business and finance, arts and entertainment, education, and families—has duped us into believing that belonging is all about being connected to people who have the same ideology as we do. This "tribalistic" perspective is not always healthy. The worldly culture separates us according to our belief systems, based on the misconception that any belief system that differs from our own threatens our fulfillment. So, we join with others and hunker down, forming our own strongholds. We forge strategic alliances based on who we reject, disagree with, or disapprove of. We see this play out daily in the media. Again and again, we're enticed to play the role of the judge, finding others guilty of not believing or behaving like us.

Today's polarized political systems casts heavy stones of shame against all who oppose its views.

Christians can act the same way and, in many respects, even worse. We separate ourselves from others in the body of Christ, based on our theological ideologies. We build walls separating "us" from "them," becoming elitist and ego-driven, judging and attacking other Christians for not holding our beliefs.

We forget that belonging to the body of Christ requires different parts working seamlessly together as one. We are unwilling to yield in humility and appreciate that others are made by God, just as he made us, and loved by God, just as he loves us. We get so caught up in the unity of opposition that we never embrace the unity of love that is available at God's table. Unity of opposition fosters a phony, super-ficial culture—an environment that keeps everyone hiding their vulnerabilities. It also fosters label-wearing for the purpose of belonging, if only to a toxic environment.

These forces, combined, create a culture of shame. Since when has God asked us to eat shame at his table? Since when has he asked us to block others from his forgiveness and cleansing of sin? To bring healing, Jesus always desires to lovingly heal mankind's vulnerabilities at the source. If we can't trust each other to be vulnerable, then how can we expect the world to come into the Church and find Jesus?

Whether we attempt to find belonging by affiliating with government, religion, education, business, or other societal segments, we're still lonely, even among the many others who affiliate with these groups. But why are we lonely within the crowd? It's because we seek belonging through these secondary sources rather than first finding belonging with ourselves and God. True belonging always starts first within ourselves. Healthy belonging happens when we embrace our vulnerabilities, accepting and loving ourselves because of them. With healthy belonging, we no longer wear phony labels in hopes of being accepted and deemed worthy of love. **Nothing destroys shame as effectively as true belonging rooted in love.**

Imagine yourself in Mephibosheth's shoes, presented with the invitation to eat at the king's table every day for the rest of your life. What a boost of self-esteem! I call that "empowerment by association." The agreement of feeling true belonging is a powerful force. In Scripture, it's called fellowship and, when it's done right, it can be very healing and transforming. The word "fellowship" is a translation of the Greek word *koinonia*, meaning association, communion, fellowship, close relationship. In this context, *koinonia* means active participation in the community through sharing of one's life and resources.

Mephibosheth is now about to experience the king's community through the sharing of the king's life and resources. It's a seat at this table for the rest of his life. Forever in fellowship, *koinonia*, with the king. Mephibosheth is forever bound to the king by association and relationship. David made a powerful oath when he said *always*. ("You will *always* eat at my table.")

What a wonderful illustration of God's grace extended through the offer of salvation! I pray that God speaks to you now as you read this, and that you understand you're always invited to the table of the King of Kings, Jesus Christ. You may be lame in both feet and come from a checkered family, or perhaps you've made mistakes you cannot let go of. But God shows you kindness. Your disabilities and vulnerabilities don't exclude you from his table. In fact, they're proof of God's ability to love you for you. He invites you to eat with him forever.

~ Table of Sustenance

Before moving to the Pacific Northwest, I lived in Las Vegas for nearly 22 years. Other than the family and friends who still live there, the only thing I miss is the cuisine. The best chefs in the world come to Las Vegas to show off their skills. One of my favorite places to eat was the Bellagio hotel and casino. It was extravagant in the greatest sense of the word. Everything served was all-you-can-eat. In other words, the food never ran out. The dining room and kitchen were always open and eager to serve guests.

Entering the dining room was an experience for all the senses. The eyes captured the beauty of the lavish banqueting tables, resplendent with luminous chandeliers and sparkling, picture-perfect place settings. The highly skilled wait staff stood at attention—ready, willing, and able to instantly fulfill any culinary request. The buffet areas featured every type of food from every part of the world. Alaskan king crab legs the length of my arm were piled high. Fruits, vegetables, desserts, and entrees I'd never seen before were there for the taking, along with every imaginable type of drink—from exotic juices and soft drinks, to every wine available on the market.

All I had to do was show my ticket, indicating I'd paid the price for admission, and take my seat at the table. I could eat and drink until I was full. (OK, *past* full!) But as wonderful as that experience was, eventually, I would become hungry and thirsty again. In the same way, in a spiritual sense, we are living in a world of so many choices and opportunities to feed ourselves. The world offers an enticing spread at its buffet table. We can pick and choose what we want, how we want it prepared, and eat as much as we like. Before long, we find ourselves sampling a little worldly belief, seasoned with a dash of dogma from our family of origin, and washed down with any "ism" we can find ... all served on a fresh bed of social media.

The result is insecurity in self, people, government, and even God. No matter how much we eat, we'll never be satisfied and we'll always leave the table with an upset stomach.

In Kings 4:38-41 (ESV), we encounter a powerful reminder of how worldly, counterfeit solutions to legitimate needs can bring calamitous results.

"Elisha returned to Gilgal and there was a famine in that region. While the company of the prophets was meeting with him, he said to his servant, 'Put on the large pot and cook some stew for these prophets.' (v. 38)

"One of them went out into the fields to gather herbs and found a wild vine and picked as many of its gourds as his garment could hold. When he returned, he cut them up into the pot of stew, though no one knew what they were. (v. 39)

"The stew was poured out for the men, but as they began to eat it, they cried out, "Man of God, there is death in the pot!" And they could not eat it. (v. 40)

"Elisha said, 'Get some flour.' He put it into the pot and said, "Serve it to the people to eat." And there was nothing harmful in the pot." (v. 41)

Just as in Elisha's times, today, we are also experiencing a famine … a spiritual famine … a crisis of scarcity on multiple fronts. And, just as the company of prophets in this story are famished, so are we. In our desperate hunger, we're willing to consume anything for the sake of feeling fulfilled. We see also that the man of God, Elisha, was preparing to provide the prophets a meal. He had a large pot heating over the fire with all the ingredients necessary for nourishment. Elisha understood his students' precarious condition and he knew how to restore their health.

In the same way, God knows exactly what you need to bring you back to health. He knows the exact causes of your symptoms—the weakness and unfulfillment that you experience. Graciously, he prepares all the right ingredients and they've been cooking in a pot just for you. However, notice verse 39 mentions one of the prophets went rogue and decided to add an unauthorized ingredient to the pot.

How often do we strike out on our own and unwittingly add something harmful to the meal God has prepared for us? Many of us have never known how to "taste and see that the Lord is good" (Psalm 34:8, NIV) because we've never allowed him to serve us a meal made from his perfect ingredients. By adding our own ideologies and worldly epiphanies—attempting to improve on the Master Chef's perfect creation—we mar the meal. In fact, it can become down-right toxic.

Rather than using our own experiences and opinions to determine what God can do in our lives, whatever happened to using the Word of God as our standard of measure? When we bypass, discard, and water down foundational truths, we're left with a Gospel message that is skewed and powerless. It brings shame to some and leaves others free to do as they please, without the convicting work of the Holy Spirit within them. They are, as described in 2 Timothy 3:2, "lovers of self," full of pride and ego, always looking to satisfy their carnal nature, appearing to be godly outwardly, but inside their "pot" is full of death.

Notice what happened to Elisha's students as they began to eat. They cried out, "Man of God, there is death in the pot!" Likewise, many of you are eating death from your pot. Maybe you've been doing your best to feed yourself, but you're never satisfied and in constant pain. All you taste is bitterness just like the wild gourd that was placed in that ancient pot. You try to blame God but you, not he, added harmful ingredients. Some of you have allowed others to add questionable things to your pot without even realizing it. Perhaps someone you trusted added toxicity that has poisoned you. No matter if it's self-inflicted or inflicted by others, the cure is the same.

In verse 41, Elisha directs the students to add flour to the pot and serve the resulting meal. Instantly, the poisonous food became healthful. In the same way, we need to add some flour into our pot. What's so special about this flour? It represents the bread of life, Jesus Christ. He is the ingredient that removes death from the pot. Jesus didn't come into the world to give bread, but to *be* bread. "I *am* the bread of life. Whoever comes to me will never go hungry" (John 6:35, NIV). "Everyone who drinks of this water will be thirsty again, but whoever drinks of the water that I will give him will never be thirsty again. The water that I will give him will become in him a spring of water welling up to eternal life" (John 4:13-14, ESV). Our souls hunger and thirst for something only God can satisfy. He gave us this hunger and thirst and, with it, he has provided a spectacular dining experience beyond all measure.

God's table always provides a Holy Communion cuisine. Communion is the sharing of intimate thoughts and feelings, especially when the exchange is on a mental or spiritual level. It is a divine exchange. The bread of communion represents Jesus' body that was scourged and broken during His crucifixion. The cup represents His shed blood. It is the life force of God—the Alpha, the Omega, the Beginning, and the End. In fact, it is the very DNA of God, commingled with yourself as you partake.

The communion meal is transformative, a divine exchange that took place on the cross. It was, and *still is*, a spiritual, supernatural event. Yet we water it down, making it into the image of man's imperfections rather than a reflection of God's absolute, loving, perfection. It is tempting to believe that the shame and mistakes from our sin remain more powerful than the broken body and shed blood of God's Son.

In embracing this lie, we remove the "super" from the "natural" and ingest a meal with no power or divine exchange. Yet the word of God fully displays his supernatural influence on our lives. Paul tells us, "And my God will meet all your needs according to the riches of his glory in Christ Jesus" (Philippians 4:19, ESV). If you want to experience riches, they are revealed at the king's table. Look no further than the supernatural, finished work of Jesus Christ on the cross. The king is sharing his life and resources with you!

When I lived in Las Vegas, I had to pay for a seat at the table in order to enjoy an extravagant meal. But, as a believer, Jesus has already paid the price for my seat. ALL are welcome when they come by faith in Jesus Christ. I urge you to trust in Jesus and humbly accept your assigned seat at the king's table, fully believing it has been prepared just for you, and for this divine moment in your life. Eat of the meal that sets you free from the mouth of shame. You may have put something harmful in your pot and others may have done so, too. No matter the cause, when we've fully ingested the spiritual meal of the finished work of Jesus, a divine exchange begins. In fact, seven exchanges take place as we dine with Christ.

1. Jesus was punished that we might be forgiven. (Isaiah 53:6, Romans 5:1)
2. Jesus was wounded that we might be healed. (Isaiah 53:4, 1 Peter 2:24)
3. Jesus was made sin that we might be made righteous. (2 Corinthians 5:21, Isaiah 53:10)
4. Jesus died our death that we might receive His life. (Romans 6:23)
5. Jesus bore our shame that we might share His glory. (Hebrews 12:2)
6. Jesus endured our rejection that we might have His acceptance with the Father. (Matthew 27:46, 50, Ephesians 1:5–6)
7. Jesus was made a curse that we might enter into the blessing. (Galatians 3:13–14, Deuteronomy 21:23)

I have witnessed many times the power of Jesus performing this divine exchange before my eyes. Many years ago, for instance, I was leading a communion service in a small Central California church, in memory of Jesus' finished work on the cross. We didn't even have the elements to offer the congregation. All we had were a few slices of wheat bread and some water. As we passed out the elements and began to pray, a holy hush came over the entire church. I knew in an instant, the Ancient of Days, the Lord God Almighty, had entered in with us. It was as if he was also honoring his Son with us.

We all smiled and wept from some place very deep inside. Not out of pain or agony, but out of gratefulness. We understood the exchange that was made and the extravagant price that was paid on the cross for each of us. We recognized how grateful God was to have us for himself and the pride he had in his Son for doing the work that brought us to the Father. Our worship began to erupt from places that had been locked up our entire lives. The freedom burst forth in everyone and every single one of those seven exchanges was exhibited that day. It was a day of miracles and not one person left unchanged. That experience taught me of my worth in the eyes of my Heavenly Father. He paid the highest price because we are worth it to Him.

Let's circle back to the beginning of this chapter and remember how king David spoke his promises to Mephibosheth. David extended his absolute grace and unmerited favor. This day, God's grace is offering you the very same thing:

Do not be afraid.
I will surely show you kindness.
I will restore to you.
You will always eat at my table.

Find a moment to take communion and reflect on this divine exchange. His "grace is sufficient for you" (2 Corinthians 12:9, ESV).

~ Resetting Your Table

Most of this chapter's content was inspired by an experience I had many years ago. I was praying for God to spiritually awaken Portland, Oregon, where I currently live. As I prayed, I began to envision a large table with many dining utensils piled high. Many more utensils than what was useful or necessary were scattered about. The knives, forks, and spoons were ugly, dingy, and grey. They'd been tossed carelessly on the table in front of each place setting, piled high in all directions.

As I looked more closely, I noticed that, underneath this mess, were beautiful goblets, and plates with gleaming forks, knives, spoons, and bowls, perfectly aligned. It was a flawless setting. To my dismay, the dingy, grey, utensils completely covered most of these flawless tableware. Only a small remnant of the beautiful, heavenly place setting could be seen beneath the clutter. Then, all at once, a giant hand appeared and swiped across the table, clearing everything with a loud crash. With that, the beautiful table settings, once barely visible, were set back on the table in their original splendor. I began to laugh, feeling overwhelmed with joy. Without any words, I understood exactly what God was showing me: We have already been given an flawless place at the king's table. Our job is simply to "Taste and see that the Lord is good" (Psalm 34:8).

You have been selected for a great culinary experience. Everything has been meticulously prepared for you, personally, down to the finest detail, by the greatest chef of all time. He knows what you like and dislike and what makes you completely fulfilled. The ambiance of this dining experience was tailored specifically to bring you joy and uplift you. However, to aid your nourishment and fulfillment, have you allowed the world's culture to place in your hands its utensils and serving dishes, which were not designed to feed you this meal? How many times have you come to the table with something else in our hand, in hopes of being able to reach fulfillment, only to leave again still hungry, thirsty, and more unfulfilled?

The very table that had been designed to bring fulfillment has been converted into a table of heartsickness, disappointments, hopelessness, and shame. God never planned to serve us emptiness at his table. My prayer is that you will recognize, right now, the bounty that is available to you at the king's table in Jesus' matchless name! I hope you will partner with the Holy Spirit and let Him reset the table of your understanding and truly taste and see that the Lord is good. Give Him permission to wipe clean everything that is harmful. Let Him wipe away, layer by layer, the false ideologies and disappointments that have always left you feeling ashamed, incomplete, and unfulfilled.

Our brother, Mephibosheth's, story reminds me of this invitation to sit at God's table. You belong at this table. You are accepted as your true self. You don't need to play dress up to dine at this table. The only requirement is enough faith in Jesus to hand over your vulnerabilities. Surrender is the catalyst that produce the divine exchange. You give Jesus your shame and he gives you the finished work of Christ. It is time to uncover your truth and live a fulfilled life as God intended. It is time to fully experience everything he has prepared for your life now in this moment. It's never too late to pull up a chair and sit with the king.

~ Prayer ~

Lord Jesus, thank you for your grace. I will choose to push past fear because I know your grace is on my life. I thank you that, in your grace, I am given loving-kindness and acceptance from your heart. It is this loving-kindness that restores my life and allows me to have a place at the table beside you. Thank you for Your amazing grace, Lord.
Amen.

Cast Off That Dead Dog!

*"The reason we struggle with insecurity is because
we compare our behind-the-scenes with
everyone else's highlight reel."*
~ Steven Furtick

Mephibosheth bowed down and said, "What is your servant, that you should notice a dead dog like me?" (2 Samuel 9:8, NIV). Every time I read this passage it breaks my heart. Notice Mephibosheth's response and how he sees himself as "a dead dog." The *Merriam-Webster* dictionary defines *dead dog* as "something no longer important."

As I think back about the years when I lived in a Lo Debar state of mind, I can relate to this concept. Many of us continuously rehash our story in our head—the story that "I'm not good enough." My inner narrative for many years was that I was unworthy to teach God's word, write books, and train others to break shame and take God's fulfillment for their lives. I re-played in my head the narratives of all the people in my life who'd said I wasn't smart enough, talented enough, or educated enough. I replayed all the times I fell flat on my face for everyone to see.

Over the years, as God has used me to work with people to change their lives, I've found that unworthiness is one of the most common of all inner narratives. We're prone to feeling unworthy of compliments; of unleashing our creativity and gifts into the world; of assuming roles of leadership; and of enjoying success, happiness, and peace. Most of all, we feel unworthy of love and acceptance. It's so easy for us to believe we're not enough to overcome our toughest struggles, to change our addictions, or conquer bad habits. We believe we're not good enough for others to know our true selves and accept us. **The mouth of shame will always tell us we are not enough.** In this state of mind, we begin to expect nothing good because that's the way our narrative has always been. It's a defeated state of existence, deep inside, that we desperately try to hide from everyone in the world.

Like Mephibosheth, we carry a dead dog mentality. It smells horrible and we do whatever it takes to hide it and mask the stench. Many of us live our entire lives as if we're all in a giant masquerade party. We rarely, if ever, remove our mask for fear of revealing the dead dog within.

We use three types of masks to hide our unworthiness: the mask of perfection, the mask of numbness, and the mask of deferred hope. In reality, more than three masks exist but, over the years, I've learned that these three are the most common. So, let's take a closer look at each one.

~ The Mask of Perfection

Perfection is a very common mask. It's a self-destructive, highly addictive belief system that tells us: if we look perfect and do everything perfectly, people will find us worthy of love and acceptance. Perfectionism is the belief that, if I am perfect, others won't see how small and unworthy I am. It's striving for the appearance of flawlessness to avoid facing our flawed selves. It's an unattainable ideal that sets excessively high standards and overly critical evaluations of ourselves and others. Instead of striving for excellence in hopes of mastering a challenge, we strive for perfection because it's the only way we can mask our feelings of unworthiness.

This mask gives us a false sense of worth when we wear it—shallow, surface worth because the mask is cursed, and so is its wearer. The curse perfectionism's mask imparts is *disappointment.* There is no such thing as a perfect person, so we ultimately set ourselves up for disappointment. We strain ourselves by exerting massive energy to uphold impossible ideals. But, no matter how hard we work, we slip and fall. Everyone does.

Perfectionists go to extraordinary lengths to maintain their façade. But the longer their mask is in place, the further away they push people who might get close enough to discover their authentic self. It's lonely and exhausting, and it eats away at their true sense of self. Perfectionists build a counterfeit identity and lose connection with who they really are.

Many Christians live in communities that require religious perfectionism. Nobody is real with each other and transparency is taboo. "Fake it till we make it" is their unspoken doctrine. They hide behind the mask of perfection to receive social acceptance from leaders and peers. Likewise, many Christian parents have handed perfectionism down to their children, who learn early that, to be accepted and found worthy of love, they must play the perfectionism game.

I pray that the Holy Spirit will give you the courage to remove the perfectionist mask and put on God's grace in Jesus' name. To be set free from wearing the mask of perfectionism, you have to cross the rickety bridge from "What will people think of me?" to "I am enough." One way to do this is to develop grace and self-compassion. Learn to be kind to yourself. Recognize that others struggle, too. Become mindful, acknowledging painful feelings without letting them take over. Accept that you are enough and God's grace is sufficient to enable you to remove the mask of perfectionism … and keep it off.

~ The Mask of Numbness

Numbing is a mask that seeks to deaden the discomfort and pain of shame. It's the "retreat and hide" coping mechanism, which is why I call this mask the turtle shell. At the first sign of pain, those who wear the numbness mask retreat deep inside to escape traumas and threats from the outside world. This shell becomes their sanctuary, hiding place, and escape from reality.

For some of us, the numbing shell might include alcohol, drugs, or sex; but, for most of us, it's less obvious. Busyness, overeating, overworking, over shopping, and spending inordinate time engaged with screens (TV, video games, phones, laptops, etc.) can all be used to numb. These behaviors are subtle because they're woven within our daily lives.

Don't get me wrong: any one of these activities in small doses is perfectly fine. But when we allow these things to become our shell, our hiding place, then our lives become ensnared. We're no longer working to overcome the challenges of life and to reach our fulfillment. Nor are we changing the thinking, behaviors, or emotions that created anxiety within us. Instead, we've become isolated and imprisoned within our own misery.

The numbing mask fights to avoid the painful anxiety and disconnection that shame brings. Shame Breakers and Fulfillment Makers cultivate the habit of facing their uncomfortable feelings and exploring their origins. Try to change the behaviors that cause overwhelming feelings, rather than simply managing the feelings by disengaging and retreating into the turtle shell.

Setting boundaries and creating an environment of accountably is a formula for freedom. Realistic boundaries include recognizing when to say enough is enough. Ask the Holy Spirit to become your hiding place and give you the courage to stop numbing and hiding your emotions.

~ Mask of Deferred Hope

Mephibosheth wears a mask I call "deferred hope." It's the mask that hides wearers from the risk of being hurt by disappointment. With this mask, even when all is going well, we fear that disaster is around the next corner. We dread what might happen next, extinguishing any hope that we might otherwise feel. The problem is, if we're not open to hope's vulnerability, that ominous dread called "fear" falls over us like a suffocating cloud. It smothers all hope and the possibility of joy that comes with it. It's the mindset that says, "Expect the worst so you won't be disappointed." But, as we read in Proverbs 13:12, "Hope deferred makes a heart sick."

Let me ask you a question. What is the worst kind of thief? The answer is the kind that steals your time, because you will never get it back. You can get your money back, your job back and even your marriage back, but time you can never get back. Once it's gone, it's gone. The mask of deferred hope is shame's master thief and its job is to steal your time in addition to your hope and joy. (That's quite a heist, right?) When good times come, you're unable to recognize them because deferred hope keeps you fixated on the possibility of what might go wrong in the future.

I remember one year I'd trained several months to fight at the Western Regionals Open karate tournament in Laughlin, Nevada. There were about 30 competitors in my division and I fought my way to first place. You would think I'd have been overjoyed by receiving that huge trophy. But, deep down inside, I was wearing the mask of deferred hope. Someone had made an off-hand comment that, "Back in the day, there would have been a hundred people in your division. You had it easy." Based on that comment, I saw my new title through the lens of shame. That lens was the agreement I'd made with myself years earlier, that I was not good enough or accepted.

Shame always tries to rob today of all its precious moments and memories. It forces you to view life through the lens of unworthiness. A perfectly celebration-worthy event can be twisted into a shameful sham by this time-stealing thief. As we wait for the other Lo Debar shoe to drop, today's good times slip away, unnoticed and unrecoverable.

In the world of economics, a related term is "scarcity." Scarcity is the state of being in short supply, fostering the fear that availability is not enough to meet the demand. During the Great Depression in the 1920s, the economy was completely decimated. There were no jobs, no food, no provision, even for the most basic needs. A whole generation grew up during this era and never fully recovered from their traumatic years of lack. Even as the economy recovered, jobs returned, and food was back on the table, something was missing. Security. Fear, panic, and anxiety—that the bottom could, again, drop out at any time—kept Depression survivors from enjoying their new-found plenty. A scarcity mindset overruled reality.

A grandfather of a friend of mine grew up during those difficult times. He was a good man who worked hard and provided for his family with a great job. He owned a house and a car. You could say he had everything that we call the American dream. Yet, deep inside, he couldn't enjoy it because he feared his money and resources might suddenly evaporate. He thought that, around the next corner, disaster was waiting to strike.

After his death, relatives discovered that he'd hidden large sums of money inside the walls of his garage. He never told a soul, not even his own family. With great remorse, his adult children reflected on all the things they were denied while growing up because the family lived on such a meager income. They thought about how much better their childhood years might have been had their father not lived as though his resources were always in short supply.

In the same way, we can be ruled by a scarcity mindset, a hope-deferred state of mind just like Mephibosheth and his dead dog mentality. When we filter our moments of blessings through the filter of negative experiences, what comes out on the other end is scarcity. To be free from the mask of hope deferred, it's vitally important to have an attitude of gratitude—a state of thankfulness to God for even the little things we have.

It's also important to remember that God supplies all our needs according to the riches of His glory in Christ Jesus (Philippians 4:19). Take time each day to thank God in all things. If your mind and heart are appreciatively focused on what you have, you'll always enjoy when more comes your way. If you concentrate on what you don't have, you'll never recognize or experience the blessings that are sent your way. I pray that, if you wear this mask of hope deferred, you will take it off and replace it with thankfulness and gratitude toward our Heavenly Father.

~ Take Off the Mask and Put on Love

The most important factor needed to live triumphantly and stop hiding behind masks, is becoming a person who is intentional and courageous in love. Love is the great eradicator of fear and small self-worth. When you courageously step out in love and view life as an opportunity to give and receive love, then—and only then—will you reach the fulfillment God desires for you. Taking off the mask and putting on love isn't easy. In many ways, I would even say it's impossible. Sure, you may experience the feelings that we label as love … that intense emotional connection. But what happens when emotions fail and the intensity you once felt is gone? God's love is so much greater than your emotional framework of what the world labels as love.

Let's examine what love looks like based on an eye-opening biblical passage, 1 Corinthians 13:4-8 (ESV), which says: "Love is patient and kind; love does not envy or boast; it is not arrogant or rude. It does not insist on its own way; it is not irritable or resentful; it does not rejoice at wrongdoing, but rejoices with the truth. Love bears all things, believes all things, hopes all things, endures all things. Love never ends."

Based on God's definition, our chances of living lives characterized by true love are dim. We might as well be attempting to climb Mt. Everest with a swim suit and a beach towel! It's impossible for us to love this way when drawing from our own abilities and strengths. This love is supernatural and far beyond the grasp of humanity in its own power. The only way for us to love, to any degree, is to know his love first.

The process of loving God's way begins when we agree with His love and then receive it. We can't give what we don't have. We receive from the Lord in the same way that people in the Bible received from the Lord… by FAITH. Our faith can have an amazing grip to hold and take what is offered from our loving heavenly father. This fact is emphasized in James 1:5–7, which tells us what to do if we are lacking something in our life. The Apostle James said that we are to ask of God, but instructs us to ask in faith in order to receive. Here and now let's receive this love as God describes. You will notice next to the sixteen attributes of God's love, below, is the word "receive." Now, clear your mind, focus on God's perfect love, read each of these descriptions, and receive:

1. Patient   (Receive)
2. Kind   (Receive)
3. Does not envy   (Receive)
4. Does not boast   (Receive)
5. It is not arrogant   (Receive)
6. It is not rude   (Receive)
7. Does not insist on
   its own selfish way   (Receive)
8. It is not irritable   (Receive)

9. It is not resentful   (Receive)

10. It does not rejoice
    in wrong-doing   (Receive)

11. It rejoices with
    the truth   (Receive)

12. It bears all things   (Receive)

13. It believes all things   (Receive)

14. It Hopes all things   (Receive)

15. It endures all things   (Receive)

16. Love never ends   (Receive)

Form healthy agreements in your mind on how God loves you. God is not selfish; John 3:16 proves that. He sent His only Son to die as a selfless act of love. He loves you so much that the highest price was paid, because He knows you are worth it. **Receiving healthy love from God is the only way we can love others as God loves us.** Yes, you will fall short and mess up, but that is when you rely on the love of God and keep trying.

For years, I hid behind a mask as a desperate attempt to prove I was tough—tough enough not to need love. But the truth was that I did need it. In fact, I craved it continually. I was in pain from negative experiences that relationships had taught me. I grew up in a very selfish, maybe even a narcissistic, environment. From an early age, I was immersed in a take,

take, take mentality. I lived in a home where tunnel vision for self-interest created a blind spot for seeing or valuing the interests of others. From this background, I formed harmful agreements … one being that only the strong and forceful get what they want in life, and nothing, or no one, else mattered. I thought this mindset was normal; it was all I knew.

Based on those experiences, I acted out what I believed love was supposed to be. I had dropped so many people who trusted me, who loved me. Sure, the emotion of love may have been there, but the selfless giving that real love produces was lacking. Many relationships laid dead in my wake, and each one left me even more discouraged and angry. The stones of shame I'd amassed in my backpack took a heavy toll. The more failed relationships I experienced, the more I telegraphed to the world that I didn't need love.

It's interesting how the very things we desire most are sometimes the things we push away most forcefully. Isn't that how this worldly culture trains us? For many, our experiences and lessons in love have been wounding experiences. As noted in Chapter 7, many of us have been dropped by someone whom we trusted, even loved. Perhaps, like me, you are the one who did the dropping; maybe dropping is part of your mask.

Did the fear of exposing the real you and being rejected for it cause you to reject others first? If so, it's time to put away the fear and put on love.

We must find the strength from the Holy Spirit to courageously love. Take off the mask, with its misguided efforts to protect you, and bravely say, "I need love and desire connection again!"

Some of you might have had the opposite of my experience. Perhaps you've chased love and given love to everyone ... but yourself. It's self-love that you have a difficulty with. If you can muster the courage to love, you'll discover that it's only a matter of time before you find the freedom you're looking for. Self-love is not ungodly, as some religious people preach. God doesn't want you to hate yourself. God desires to give you good things because He loves you and knows your worth. You are worth so much more than a dead dog. Jesus paid the ultimate price for your freedom. He willingly gave His own life ... for YOU!

So, begin to love yourself, respect yourself, nurture yourself, and honor yourself because God does the same toward you. He is calling you away from wearing those destructive masks.

You must honor the person you are in Jesus Christ. Cast off the dead dog mentality and the mask that hides it. Recognize that you are worthy of the invitation to His table. This awareness is healing to your wounds and fosters communion between you and God. If you honor yourself with love, understanding that God desires you to be loved, then everything will begin to change for you in marvelous ways. When you practice giving love, and accept the kindness and love of others, it is so healing.

This is why getting into the Word of God it vitally important. His Word is the soil in which the seeds of love will thrive as they take root. We know His Word takes root when we are able to live a life of love in action. Every action of love then becomes worship, in which we are honoring God in ourselves. Remember, you are not a dead dog. You are God's object of lovingkindness and every flaw is embraced by Him with love. So, I challenge you, kick off the dead dog mentality, rip off the mask you have been hiding behind, and have the courage to put on love.

~ Prayer ~

Lord Jesus please help me to recognize if I am hiding behind a mask. I ask that you remove the desire of covering up my vulnerabilities. I want to be free from the fear of not being good enough. I ask that you help me wear your love. Give me confidence to love others and myself in a deliberate way. I now choose to take off the mask and put on your love.

Amen.

God Prepares You in Private to Reveal You in Public

"When God created you, He created a dream and wrapped a body around it."
~ Lou Engle

"And the king called to Ziba, Saul's servant, and said to him, 'I have given to your master's son all that belonged to Saul and to all his house. You therefore, and your sons and your servants, shall work the land for him, and you shall bring in the harvest, that your master's son may have food to eat. But Mephibosheth your master's son shall eat bread at my table always.' Now Ziba had fifteen sons and twenty servants. Then Ziba said to the king, 'According to all that my lord the king has commanded his servant, so will your servant do …'" (2 Samuel 9: 9-11).

God prepares you in private to reveal you in public. He turns tragedy into triumph and tests into testimonies. This is how the message of the Gospel is spread and the glory of God is released on the earth.

We all have a story to tell, and God has a book with all your days recorded into it (Psalm 139:16). Also recorded in this book are the dreams God has for your life, plans to prosper you, not to harm you, to give you hope, and a bright future (Jeremiah 29:11). You are designed to prosper and to be fulfilled by the author of all life.

Yet, we possess a powerful faculty, given to all humanity, called *free will*. We can choose to take the pen from the author's hand and write our own story, or we can trust the Creator and let him complete our pages, surrendering the pen to him and partnering with him to become the person we were designed to be. Every one of us has a promise over our life and whether, we realize it or not, it is there for the taking.

As I write this, I know some of you are struggling to hold onto the promise of fulfillment that God has for you. Some of you have been given a prophetic word, a promise from God for your life, and you formed an agreement with it. That promise began to grow inside you, much like a baby. At that moment, God's dream also became your dream. Then, tragedy, challenges, and difficulties knocked you off your feet. Discouragement set in and the dream started to fade away.

Satan will always do whatever he can to abort God's dreams for your life. The Enemy's strategy is simple and effective: discourage you, slay any hope you have for a better future, and, above all, convince you to retrieve the pen from God's hand. Holding you back from living God's dream for you is important to Satan because you, in Christ, are a threat to everything he is trying to build in this world. **When we live our lives according to God's plan, we each become a wrecking ball to the kingdom of darkness.**

To thwart the Enemy's plan, you must hold onto the reality that God is about your growth and prosperity in Him. The person who plants a seed in the ground cannot expect to reap an immediate harvest. A process must unfold. The time between when the seed is planted and when the crop is harvested—what I call the "in-between time"—represents an epic battle ground. If Satan can get you to quit in the in-between time, you'll be stuck in unfulfillment and miss your breakthrough into blessing. Have faith when you can't yet see the fruit of God's promises in your life. It's on its way! And, as you wait, remember: "He who is in you is greater than he who is in the world" (1 John 4:4, NKJV).

Just as God gives us specific promises about things he dreams for our lives, planting those promises in our hearts, we can dream along with God for the fulfillment of his plans. However, many times we are not at a place to handle the blessing yet. The growth has to happen before the harvest can take place. The person we are when God gives us a promise, in many cases, is not the same person as when the promise is fulfilled. **There must always be growth and transformation to be strong enough to handle the blessing and promises of God.** A wisdom key to remember is that the pressures of life produce the growth. Some give up and lose heart. But I want to encourage you to be patient in affliction (Romans 12:12). Let the Holy Spirit partner with you, using affliction to your advantage. You are not alone and your story is unfolding. Do not let Satan knock you off course and into the land of in-between.

By the time we meet Mephibosheth in 2 Samuel, he has lived through much hardship. Imagine the years of heartache and solitude, watching his able-bodied friends and family enjoying their lives while he languished—despised and immobilized. Do you ever feel that way? Perhaps you're watching others live "the good life" while your life is a mess. You feel like opportunity and blessing have avoided you like a teenager asked to do dirty dishes. I imagine that was Mephibosheth's experience. He thought his best days were behind him … like he'd drawn the short straw and lost … never realizing the hard times served in the depths of Lo Debar were part of a fantastic process to demonstrate God's power on display. He had no way of knowing that his years of intense anguish and despair would reveal a story that would bless the world by revealing the salvation message of God. We all have a story to tell of our times in Lo Debar. Many of us have gone through hard, even horrific, moments. I want to remind you of God's unfailing promise to bring you into a place of hope and purpose.

~ The Mighty Olive

If there is one symbol that fully depicts the private season of a Fulfillment Taker, it's the olive. From an ordinary olive, God produces tremendous blessing. Since the times of Genesis until today, the olive has been used for remarkable things. It has no outward beauty like many other fruits, and it tastes bitter when plucked off the tree. It's not large and it even has a pit inconveniently situated in its center.

Yet, despite its drawbacks, the olive is replete with benefits. For instance, it produces fine oil. In the Old Testament, God always ordained the anointing oil to bless His people, transforming the ordinary into something extraordinary. This practice carried over into the New Testament as the anointing oil speaks of Christ and His finished work. Understanding this symbolism will give you access to God's supernatural provision of wholeness and victorious living. The Bible doesn't teach that anointing oil is a magic potion, like something a witch would use to cast a spell. No, I'm describing the power of Jesus Christ at work in us who believe. While entire books have been dedicated to this topic, I want to briefly touch on how olive oil is made, which symbolizes the very process of victorious living.

~ The Process of Anointing

The transformation process of the small, insignificant, bitter olive into precious, valuable oil is God's perfect illustration of how he can transform our lives into something extraordinary. The transformative power of God at work within us is much like the olive press of old.

To make oil, the olive had to be crushed under extreme weight by a giant stone. If the olive is pressed lightly, very little oil will come from it and the olive's innate bitterness will transfer to the oil. The oil's quality and purity are based on the pressure and time spent under the olive press, allowing each olive to produce, in oil, its full potential. In the same way, we must yield our lives to the daily pressures that God, our rock, permits to bear down on us. In this life, we will always face pressures. We can try and handle them, ourselves, and produce very little, if any, value from our efforts. Or, we can submit to the pressure exerted by the Rock of Our Salvation, Jesus Christ.

I sometimes wonder why the world has so many bitter Christians. Could it be because our transformation process has been halted? Have we stopped pressing in to God, our rock? Only he can press out the bitterness and bring forth the quality of oil and anointing available within us. We cannot afford to allow the discomfort of the process to outweigh the hope of being fully and uniquely transformed into the image of Christ (Romans 8:29), which God desires.

You are not alone! We have all been there. And I want to you know: God's Word contains accounts of many people who were of no reputation, just like an olive, and who went on to produce precious, valuable oil as they patiently yielded to God's sovereign press.

~ God's Anointing Transforms

When King David acted with kindness toward Mephibosheth, the results were liberating. The king blessed Jonathan's son in front of the people of his past. Remember, Ziba served Mephibosheth's family while his grandfather, Saul, was king. David made a point to honor and bless Mephibosheth in front of Ziba. Nothing is more freeing than finding honor after you've lost it, or gaining it for the first time after never having experienced it before.

One of the first things shame steals is your sense of honor. What is honor? *Merriam-Webster* defines it as:

a: good name or public <u>esteem</u>:
REPUTATION

b: a showing of usually <u>merited </u>respect:
RECOGNITION

Notice the theme here: "*a good name*." In Mephibosheth's case, we begin to see that a good name is replacing the name from the mouth of shame. He is shedding the old label that shame tried to stick on him. Remember, shame will call you by your disabilities, but God calls you by your abilities. This truth is perfectly demonstrated in this passage. Wherever you find honor, you find a good reputation. One cannot exist without the other. The king is conferring a good reputation upon our brother Mephibosheth ... restoring, in the eyes of his past and present community members, the reputation of one who was once considered no more valuable than a dead dog.

Public shame can tarnish anyone's reputation. Our worldly culture has trained society members to watch in fascination as targeted victims are devastated by it. Marvelously, God is the rebuilder of reputations. Throughout the Bible, God demonstrates his restoration power. Here are a number of examples:

1. **Jacob** carried the reputation as a deceiver and a liar, but God made him into a blessing for generations and named him Israel.

2. **Moses** had a reputation as an orphaned boy who had speech difficulties and was a murderer. God made him a leader and the deliverer of Hebrew slaves from Egypt.

3. **Joseph's** reputation problems started when he was rejected by his brothers. He was then enslaved and, eventually, imprisoned. But God placed Joseph in charge of everything in Egypt—second only to Pharaoh.

4. **Gideon** was a fearful man who lived in hiding. God made him into a warrior who led a small-but-mighty army to deliver Israel from Median's hands. What a reputation turnaround we see in his amazing story!

5. **The Apostle Paul** (before he became the writer of most of the New Testament books) was Saul of Tarsus. He earned a reputation by terrorizing the early church. Not only was he present when Stephen, the first Christian martyr, was killed, but Paul heartily approved of the murder.

6. **Peter** denied Jesus while he was arrested and tortured, but Peter also was the first of the twelve apostles to whom Jesus appeared. He restored Peter in a touching moment on the shores of the Sea of Galilee. Peter then went on to become the leader of the disciples, preaching the first evangelical message after which more than 3,000 people were saved.

7. **Deborah** stepped into a position previously held only by men. She restored the reputation

of women. Before Israel had kings, they looked to judges to lead them. The nation was led to freedom through her leadership. She did not let the culture of the world define her life because she was a woman. She proved women are mighty in the Lord and showed us that, just because something hasn't been done before, doesn't mean you shouldn't do it.

8. **Esther** was adopted by her cousin, Mordecai. Their bond led her to marry a king. She orchestrated the rescue of all the Jewish people in Persia. Along the way, her reputation—from poor orphan to royal freedom-fighter—was restored.

9. **Mary Magdalen**e was delivered by Jesus of demons and became one of his closest followers. She started with a reputation as being unclean, but God restored her and she became a financial supporter and follower of Jesus' ministry. She was also a witness to Christ's crucifixion and she was present at his burial. All four Gospels identify her as being the first to witness Jesus' empty tomb and the first to witness his resurrection. Many scholars call her the Apostle to the Apostles.

These individuals represent just a handful of biblical accounts of God restoring tarnished reputations. Each story proves that the **only way a defamed reputation can have the last word in our lives is if we choose to let it.** We serve a God who is able to take our defeats, missteps, and shame, and use us to bring glory to His Name. He brings beauty from the ashes (Isaiah 61:3, NIV) of life's unfortunate events. And he is still restoring reputations today.

~ My Broken Reputation

Earlier, I shared how I adopted the shameful reputation others gave me during my difficult teen years. I formed agreements within myself regarding who I was and I acted those agreements out. Everyone said I was a bad seed and so I became that person. I had no compassion and didn't care about people or life beyond what would benefit me. I used people and became very good at it. Intimacy, for me, created vulnerability and being vulnerable was terrifying. Therefore, I erected outer armor to help protect my inner self and ensure I got what I needed.

I lived in a fog that I called survival mode. It was a way of life that was so self-absorbing, I didn't recognize anyone else. Perpetually lonely, I destroyed good relationships that I regret to this day. I didn't know how to let anyone come close enough emotionally to discover the real me and I didn't even know who the real Tony was. I had spent so many years in hiding behind this disguise; it was all I knew.

I was not only trying to protect myself, but also attempting to remake my identity. I thought that, since I'd already been rejected, maybe I could pretend to be someone else to gain the world's acceptance and feel fulfilled. To make matters worse, I was always changing my disguise to fit into whatever situation or season I happened to be in. Like a chameleon, I changed my colors so many times that I forgot what my original color looked like. It was a massive identity crisis. Angry and deceitful, the only constant in life was the pain of who I was and the determination to hide from it.

Back in those days, I worked in what was called a "boiler room"—an office loaded with desks and phones. I called mostly elderly people, offering them the hope of winning prizes if they purchased a year's supply of vitamins for $700. The unsuspecting victims would send us their money and get a five-dollar prize in return. We led customers to believe they'd receive merchandise worth far more than the $700 they spent. In fact, we encouraged them to send photos of themselves with their valuable prizes so we could use them in our ad campaigns.

Many of those I solicited bought repeatedly, which gave me a nefarious idea. I began calling back all the customers from my home phone, telling them I worked for a government task force that was attempting to recoup all the swindled money. The only catch was that I needed a 10 percent retainer fee, upfront, to represent them.

I'd hit an all-time low but, instead of listening to the voice of my dimming conscience, I just kept digging. I rationalized my deeds by telling myself that the world took everything from me, so I deserved to recoup a tiny bit of what was owed me. It was such a twisted way of thinking. I took pride in my ability to skillfully pickpocket people with my words and in knowing that no one else my age had an apartment or ample cash. But my "success" was just another mask, keeping me from dealing with how I saw myself—a loser.

One evening, I turned on the local TV news and was dumbfounded to see an investigative reporter standing in front of the mail pick up center where I rented a mailbox to facilitate my fraudulent scheme. The report included an interview with the state attorney general, who said she was commissioning a full investigation. As I watched in absolute shock, family members began calling, telling me the FBI was looking for me.

My trial was publicized on the local news and I pled guilty to the charges. During my time in court, I remember hearing the words, "The United States of America versus Tony Caiazza." Those eight words broke me somewhere deep inside. It was not the pronouncement that I was going to jail; it was the fact that my own country that I loved was against me. For me, even the mask I was wearing to cover up my shame and bad reputation could not hide this deep disgrace. **I was a loser in the eyes of my nation and it was on TV for everyone to see.**

With complete sincerity, I wrote letters to the victims of my crime, apologizing for my dishonorable actions. And I paid my debt to society, spending the next year behind bars. When I gained my freedom, I began abusing drugs to help me sleep at night. Reminiscent of my childhood, I began to experience horrible "night terrors" every night. I had no doubt this disturbance resulted from a spiritual attack against me. I looked for ways to escape it. I talked with my grandmother, a devout Roman Catholic, and got no real answers. I read books on the occult and witchcraft that seemed to describe my experiences as demonic activity. My only solution was to get as high as I could every night because only then—at least most of the time—could I avoid feeling the attacks.

Then, around the Fall of 1998, I noticed things begin to feel different in my life. Some sort of shift was happening, though, at the time, I couldn't say what. A feeling of expectancy began hovering over my life as though, at any moment, something good was about to happen. It was like the changing from Winter to

Spring. Then it happened. I met a young lady named Angela.

I was eating at a community college deli where my brother worked. (I'd stop by a couple of times a week after work for the free food.) Angela strolled in sporting a beautiful smile and a baseball cap with "good girl" embroidered on it. I was immediately intrigued and struck up a conversation. It wasn't long before we fell in love … and I learned about Jesus.

Angela was a Christian and we'd spend hours talking about God. I would argue that God was a crutch for weak people and that, if God was really love, why would He let bad things happen. I wasn't used to having a relationship with a person who loved God. It was beautiful to me, and very interesting to see her faith lived out before my eyes. I fell hard and fast. I truly loved this girl!

Then one day, not long after we met, Angela dropped the bomb. She told me she was planning to move away to attend a private college back East. It was like a sucker-punch to the gut. I was devastated. Here was this wonderful person, the first good thing I had experienced since I was a kid, and she was about to walk out of my life forever. The very thought devastated me. That night, I was about to embark on my secret routine of getting high before bed but, instead, I found myself having a conversation … with God.

"God," I said haltingly, "if you're real, please keep Angela from moving away. Please have her stay here with me. If you do this, I will serve you for the rest of my life." During that brief conversation, I began talking with him, opening my heart as I shared my worries and pain. I remember, immediately, what I describe now as the peace of God completely filling me. It felt like a warm blanket that wrapped around me. I instantly fell asleep without needing to get high. I slept, safe and secure, that night for the first time in a very long time. I remember waking up the next morning with an overwhelming desire to talk with this person, God, who had given me such peace the night before.

Abruptly, and without really even understanding why, I opened my closet and felt compelled to empty everything out of it. I pulled out all my hanging garments and every shoe, piling them all in the middle of my bedroom floor. When I was finished, the closet was entirely empty. Looking back today, I realize that God was showing me my need to make room for him in the closet space of my heart. It was a physical action to match the spiritual action that was taking place. I was so determined to meet this divine person who helped me the previous night, I would have cleared a thousand closets.

When I finished, I entered my empty closet, turned off the light, and sat down. Before I could say a word, I heard a voice say to me, "I am your Father. Call me your Father." The way that I heard this voice was not like anything I had ever heard before. It was not an audible sound from my ear drums; this was on a deeper level. Every part of me heard this voice. Every part of me wanted to know this Father, whom I was now meeting in my bedroom closet.

The next day, Angela called me to say she'd reconsidered moving away to attend college. Instead, she'd be attending the university in our hometown. She explained that, after praying about the decision, she felt that God wanted her to stay and that she should be with me. I wish I could say that, from that moment forward, life was all roses, but, unfortunately, every rose has its thorns.

I was still trying to shake the mistakes and shames of my past. It was one thing to experience winning the love of my Angela, and for her to see me, behind the mask, and love me for me. However, her family's rejection served as thorns, piercing right through me and triggering my shame once again. After five years, and many struggles to win their approval, her parents begrudgingly gave their blessing for me to marry their daughter. To this day, she remains my prize and God's gift of grace over my life.

~ How God Restored My Reputation

The realization that God restores reputations began during my second year as the youth pastor with the International Church of Las Vegas. Our church partnered with the Dream Center in Los Angeles to plant a ministry and inner-city church in Las Vegas. It was led by a great, young pastor, Aaron Hansel, and his wife, Danita. We helped the poor, addicted, and homeless meet their basic needs, feeding them, clothing them, and providing after-school programs for their kids.

My restoration process began through this service. When we stop trying to be great among people and lose ourselves in serving others, we begin operating through the heart of Jesus Christ. Striving to make a reputation is a worldly culture view. The heavenly culture view involves losing your reputation by taking on the nature of a servant.

Philippians 2:3-8 NIV explains this well:

"Do nothing out of selfish ambition or vain conceit. Rather, in humility value others above yourselves. (v.3)

Not looking to your own interests but each of you to the interests of the others. (v.4)

In your relationships with one another, have the same mindset as Christ Jesus: (v.5)

Who, being in very nature God, did not consider equality with God something to be used to his own advantage; (v.6)

rather, he made himself nothing by taking the very nature of a servant, being made in human likeness. (v.7)

And being found in appearance as a man,
he humbled himself by becoming obedient to death—even death on a cross!" (v.8)

It reminds me of Jesus' words in Mathew 10:39, when he said that, to find our life, we must lose it. That was me. I was trying for so many years to earn a reputation that, in all honesty, was just another disguise. But during those first years in ministry, I was finding my new life, and losing my old one, as I became engrossed in the service of others. We opened our ministry in the heart of the toughest area in the city— a neighborhood known on the streets as "Heroin Heights"—operating out of a '50s-era abandoned hotel and casino used as a government housing project. Members of our ministry team didn't fear how bad the neighborhood was. Instead, we lost ourselves in the service of others we loved and we conducted warfare against the spiritual forces of darkness in that area.

One day, a letter arrived, addressed to the pastors of the Las Vegas Dream Center. The letter said that the city wished to honor the pastors for the work we were doing in the North Las Vegas community. They asked if we'd be willing to open their City Council meeting in prayer. At the time, I figured Aaron would do the honors because I was just a youth pastor. However, he said he'd be out of town and that he wanted me to attend and represent the Center.

The evening of the City Council meeting, my wife and I drove to the North Las Vegas City Hall. As I approached the building, I recognized it. It was the place I was incarcerated 7 years prior. I noticed my hands were sweating and my heart was beating fast. I began to relive those troubled times in my head. I pictured myself wearing a tan jump suit and shower shoes—the clothing the inmates wore in that facility. Fear was creeping in and I began to panic inwardly.

"What are you doing here, *convict*?" asked the mouth of shame in full attack mode. Part of me wanted to turn around and drive home. But then, I felt a boldness well up inside, clearing out every room that shame was beginning to occupy. The voice yelled, "You lose, Devil! Tonight, God gets the glory and he is sharing the victory with me!"

I remember walking into the City Council meeting as they introduced me as "Tony Caiazza, Pastor with the Dream Center of Las Vegas." Immediately the awareness came to me. I used to be announced as the "United States of America versus Tony Caiazza," but God had restored my reputation and I was now being honored and recognized for good things. Through the heart of Jesus inside me, I opened the meeting with a fervent prayer of blessing and wisdom. Weeks later, a letter arrived thanking me, on behalf of the city, for the passionate prayer and welcoming me back any time. If God can elevate my reputation—from Lo-Debar to the king's table—he can do it for you, too. Romans 2:11 teaches us that he doesn't play favorites.

I wish I could say that everyone in your life will see you the way God sees you and that your reputation will be restored in the eyes of every person. Unfortunately, that's not realistic. In my life, there have been people who, to this day, I have basically zero credibility with. It's those particular situations, I would like to address now.

I've heard people preach not to take things personally but it's hard not to. In fact, it's our human nature to do the exact opposite. We take everything personally. For example, let's say you see a family member every holiday and, each time you meet, he remarks about how horrible you were as a child. The resulting pain can be difficult to navigate. It's helpful to remember that the hurtful remarks have nothing to do with you and everything to do with the person who spoke them. If you take the comments too personally, you're letting someone else's opinions affect how you see yourself. Sometimes opinions bring good fruit that brings correction, encouragement and healthy perspective. Unfortunately, it's the bad fruit opinions from unqualified sources that bring so much hardship and pain in our lives. It is the unqualified sources we seek out for our own self worth that I want to expand on.

I think about the fairy tale of the woman who looked into her magic mirror saying, "Mirror, mirror, on the wall, who is the fairest of them all?" We subconsciously do this all the time. We seek validation in a reflection of others, giving them control of how we regard ourselves. We strive to base our reputations on other's opinions of who they think we are. If it were not the case, you wouldn't care what that family member says about your past. We take it personally because we desire to be approved. It's like we chase mirrors, asking, "Am I smart enough for you? Am I beautiful enough for you? Am I acceptable enough for you?" The answer in most cases is … no! Not because you are not enough or are in some way undesirable.

It's because people typically view themselves through their own flawed lens of negative experiences and false agreements. It's contagious and passed on like a virus. As soon as you form the agreement that the approval of others is more important than the reflection of how you see yourself—and how God sees you—you allow yourself to become trapped behind someone else's distorted lens and disfigured reflection of you.

In this worldly culture, many are trapped behind a reflection of shame. The entrapment is caused by personal importance. Personal importance, or taking things personally, is the maximum expression of self-ishness because we assume that everything is about us. Even if others insult you directly, it has nothing to do with you. What people think, what people say, what people do, and the opinions they share stem from the agreements they've formed in their own minds. Taking things personally makes you an easy victim, allowing others to easily hook you with one little tug of an opinion. You bring all their heavy emotional stones into your spiritual backpack and, now, their burden becomes yours. But if you learn not to take others' opinions personally, you'll become immune to the projections of the flawed reflections of others. Accomplishing this is more easily said than done. But you can do all things through Christ's strength (Philippians 4:13).

Do not be discouraged when you find yourself struggling with taking insults personally. Overcoming the negative opinions of others is a major hurdle. I wish I could say that, as I write this book, I have slayed this beast but, unfortunately, I, too, am still a work in progress. The encouraging thing is that God picks us up when we stumble and is always there to help us evolve into a better human being. We can only win when we allow the Holy Spirit to do his work within us. When we truly recognize this truth, we can be assured that we are accepted by God, whose opinion is the highest standard. All other opinions aren't worth a grain of salt compared to His.

Once we accept this truth, we're free from the need to be accepted by others. For example, my sense of worth no longer depends on someone telling me, "Tony, you're the best!" or "Tony, you don't measure up to my standards." Whatever they think, whatever they feel, I know it is their perspective, not mine. It is the way they see the world. It is nothing personal, because they are dealing with themselves, not with me. Others are going to have their own opinion according to their belief system, so nothing they think about me is really about me, but rather about them.

Your reputation should always be based on the reflection of who you are in Christ because his reflection of you is the only one that's truly valid. His reflection of you comes from a completely pure place. It's not biased or defiled by people's negative experiences that have distorted the truth about you. Your reputation is based in the reflection of your God. **Allow your maker to become your mirror, and not the world around you.**

Now, I say all of this with a healthy dose of caution. Please don't dismiss godly wisdom and counsel that others may give you. It can be your lifeline, pulling you out of the most difficult times, and a caution sign that the road you are on is hazardous. Test feedback with the Word of God. Does it help mature you in Christ, or is it a poison apple carefully designed to look healthy but, in the end, be deadly? Throughout my lifetime, I've had many speak various words over me. Some of these words have produced good things—the good fruit described in Galatians 5—but some have yielded just the opposite.

Your reputation will always be based on how you bring honor to others and, sometimes, you might get a little off course. Those are the times you need to hear the truth in love, testing it with the Word before deciding to embrace it or reject it. Who is in your inner circle of influence and able to speak into your life? Not everyone has earned this privilege. Don't allow the opinion of those who aren't in your circle of trust to affect you. Accountability is a vitally important part of our growth in Christ and ability to live a fulfilled life. We need to evaluate our relationships to determine who deserves to be in our inner circle. Who can you be vulnerable with and not wear a mask to cover up? No matter who it might be, remember the first one on your list is Jesus.

~ **Prayer** ~

Lord Jesus, I surrender my whole reputation. I hand over all the good, bad and ugliness on how I am perceived by others. Let other people's opinions no longer trigger the pain of shame and rejection in my life. Give me favor to find healthy relationships that can speak truth in love and help me to grow. I pray that where my reputation has been broken You would rebuild it again; that I would find my lost reputation within You my Lord Jesus.

Amen.

You Are More Than a Guest ... You Are Family

"In Christ we become God's sons, man's servants and the devil's masters."
~ John G. Lake

2 Samuel 9:11-13 reads:

"Then said Ziba unto the king, according to all that my lord the king hath commanded his servant, so shall thy servant do. As for Mephibosheth, said the king, *he shall eat at my table, as one of the king's sons.* (v.11)

And Mephibosheth had a young son, whose name was Micha. And all that dwelt in the house of Ziba were servants unto Mephibosheth. (v. 12)

So, Mephibosheth dwelt in Jerusalem: for he did eat continually at the king's table; and was lame on both his feet." (v. 13)

It is here we begin to see that Mephibosheth is not just being invited as a dinner guest, he is being invited into the king's family. Yet, it's still so much deeper than that! Mephibosheth's spiritual backpack is now being filled with good things. The rejection piled high from years of being an outcast is suddenly being removed and replaced with the acceptance of the king as part of his inner circle called family. Suddenly, the labels society forced him to wear are torn off. He wears a new label: *"one of the king's sons."* It says Mephibosheth is family. The mask of deferred hope is removed and the ability to hope and dream is restored.

As part of my research for this book, I listened to interviews of young adults who were orphaned as children. Each one had been placed into the foster care system. Of the 20 or so young adults interviewed, two common traits emerged regarding how they all felt and thought during those years. First, they shared a fear of never being accepted by another family. And, second, they longed to find, as one young lady said, "a once-and-for-all home." I loved that statement. "A once-and-for-all home." This is exactly how the story of Mephibosheth ends! You see, he was not just a guest, he was now family. It was a once-and-for-all command from the king. The king said always. This meant continually, constantly, and permanently.

In the same way, we have not only been given a permanent and continual place at the table with God, but we have also been adopted as His children. Belonging is the greatest medicine to a soul wounded by shame. Notice what the passage did not say. It did not say Mephibosheth was healed before being accepted at David's table as a son. No, it said he continually ate at the table and both feet were lame. God embraces our imperfections, our vulnerable, and weak places. It's time for you to break the lying agreements that you're not good enough and receive the medicine of truth that, in your flawed state, you are accepted, you are enough, and you are worthy of love. Tear away the false labels you wear upon yourself to fit in and be approved by others. Take the masks off and give yourself the approval to be at your worst and know you are loved, and have a once-and-for-all home and family.

This is the type of belonging that touches our wounded soul and brings a healing that inspires confidence to rise up, shake off the rubble from shame, and take flight into our fulfillment. You no longer need to live in the fear of being rejected or the belief that your lameness will somehow cause God to refuse you. It's time to stop trying to measure God by the limits of your own humanity. It's time to break the ancient agreements that say God is not good enough, or able enough, or does not desire us enough. Stop measuring God's love and acceptance with the same measuring rod that man uses to evaluate us. God's ways are higher than our ways, and his thoughts are always higher than our thoughts. Intellectually, it's hard to grasp heavenly things that cannot be measured, because things that can be measured are concrete. We must embrace the idea that God is much larger than what we have managed to make measurable, and that he largely exists outside the comfort zone of what is known. Only then can we begin to grasp the divine understanding of God's love and acceptance for us. You may have been dropped by someone you trusted, or you may have been the one who dropped someone else. You might feel crippled in both feet and might even need someone to carry you to your seat at God's table. But, assuredly, I tell you that you are accepted. And, just like Mephibosheth, you will always eat at the king's table as one of his children.

~ Prayer ~

Father, open the eyes of my understanding that I would know what it means to be your child and live a fulfilled life. I thank you that I am accepted as my true self because you sent Christ to rescue me. I trust Your mercy and transforming grace on my life. Thank you that I can now call You Father.

Amen.

Your Backpack Holds Unlimited Blessings

*"God has privileged us in Christ Jesus to live above
the ordinary human plane of life. Those who want
to be ordinary and live on a lower plane can
do so, but as for me, I will not."*
~ Smith Wigglesworth

Your spiritual backpack contains royalty—a bloodline that traces back more than 2000 years. It's a bloodline greater than any earthy dynasty. This bloodline is not victorious through self-exaltation or earthly fiat. This royal family does not come to be served, but to serve and give their lives as a ransom for many. They take up their cross and come after the One who did it all first. He is the One who is The Way, The Truth and the Life. He is both the Lion and the Lamb, The Alpha and The Omega. The Prince of Peace, and the Commander of Angel Armies. He is the Light of the world, the Word of God made into flesh. He is the Friend of Sinners and Captain of our Salvation. He is The Lifter of Our Head and The Strength of Our Heart. He is Our Healer and Our Deliverer. He is the one and only Christ, the Savior of the world. He has absolute power because he is power. He has absolute authority, because all authority has been granted to him. There is no greater power or authority in heaven, earth, or hell below that can defeat him. All things are subjected under his feet. He is the King of Kings and the Lord of Lords and sits at the right hand of power next to God the Father. This is the King who calls you his family member—his own child—and, make no mistake, you are to rule with him.

To be a Fulfillment Maker, you first must recognize what is available to you as a child of God. Every spiritual blessing is available to you according to the glorious riches of Jesus Christ (Ephesians 1-3). This is what fulfillment is all about. You carry the kingdom of God inside of you, the very atmosphere of his supernatural realm. Luke 17:21 says you are not only a citizen of this kingdom, but a royal family member. As family, you bring the kingdom agenda with you everywhere you go. As family, everything you do is an extension of the throne. From this throne, his children (that means you!) wield incredible power. Many passages of Scripture explain this fact and, perhaps, that will be a book in the future. But, until then, let's focus on the two main blessings that God has given you in your pack.

1. Your family birthright (sealed with fire in the power of the Holy Spirit)
2. Your family name (shared positioning into all authority)

~ Your Spiritual Birthright

The following three passages of Scripture contain much meaning as to who you really are:

"For you did not receive the spirit of slavery to fall back into fear, but you have received the Spirit of adoption as sons, by whom we cry, 'Abba! Father!'" (Romans 8:15, ESV).

"And because you are sons, God has sent the Spirit of his Son into our hearts, crying, 'Abba! Father!' So, you are no longer a slave, but a son, and if a son, then an heir through God" (Galatians 4:6-7, ESV).

"In him we have obtained an inheritance, having been predestined according to the purpose of him who works all things according to the counsel of his will, so that we who were the first to hope in Christ might be to the praise of his glory. In him you also, when you heard the word of truth, the gospel of your salvation, and believed in him, were sealed with the promised Holy Spirit, who is the guarantee (down payment) of our inheritance until we acquire possession of it, to the praise of his glory" (Ephesians 1:11-14, ESV).

It's no surprise this worldly culture is completely ignorant and has no clue about your true identity. This is why it's vital to view your reflection from God's mirror and not the world's. The powers of darkness will do anything and everything to keep you from recognizing your divine birthright—all that's available to you as a child of God. You're the true rags-to-riches story, just like Mephibosheth. You possess tremendous blessing, not only to break shame in yourself, but also in everyone around you. Your spiritual backpack is loaded with the power of God's kingdom to bring reality to earth as it is in heaven. It wasn't good enough for you to be born again. God did not leave your transformation at that. He went out of his way to show all creation that he chose you and adopted you into His family.

The greatest of adoptions are not the acts of humanity adopting humanity, but God choosing and adopting you with your imperfections and disabilities. This adoption is transformative, life altering, and a disruption to all things destructive. This adoption also comes with credentials that testify not only to your regal spiritual family, but also to your worth. The first chapter of Ephesians says you have inherited every spiritual blessing in Christ Jesus, according to His glorious riches. You have been given a deposit—a down payment—on this inheritance, which adds inestimable value to the life you are living right now.

Psalm 139:17-18 (ESV) tells us, "How precious also are Your thoughts to me, O God!

How vast is the sum of them! If I could count them, they would outnumber the sand.

When I awake, I am still with You." To try to grasp the magnitude of God's thoughts toward you, consider the following study: A group of researchers at the University of Hawaii set out to attempt to count the number of grains of sand on all the earth. These brilliant mathematical minds came up with an astounding figure. The earth contains approximately seven quintillion, five hundred quadrillion grains of sand. To grasp the magnitude, here's the Arabic numeral: 700,500,000,000,000,000,000.

Now imagine: God thinks of you even more than all that sand! And not just any thoughts; these are precious, good thoughts. Try and squeeze all of those thoughts into your minimal concept of time and you'll begin to understand that he has been thinking of you since before the foundations of the earth. God is intentional towards you. He is calculated and premeditated in creating your fulfillment. You are a dream that God has been carefully planning. **You are destined for greatness with a spiritual backpack loaded full of the kingdom of God.** It's no accident you are here in this world. You were born for a divine purpose as a child of the Most High God. You carry (even now) in your backpack, a deposit, a down payment, of the fullness of the blessing that is to come. This deposit, given to you now, is the Holy Spirit. He is alive and full of power and fire—a direct promise from God our Father. Let's examine these next three Scriptures to find out more about the Spirit's work:

"I baptize you with water for repentance. But after me comes one who is more powerful than I, whose sandals I am not worthy to carry. He will baptize you with the Holy Spirit and fire" (Matthew 3:11, NIV). We read here that John the Baptist foretold that Jesus is going to baptize us with his Holy Spirit and fire. Later, in Luke, Jesus speaks to his disciples about this again, saying he would be sending that promise to them.

"I am going to send you what my Father has promised; but stay in the city until you have been clothed with power from on high" (Luke 24:49, NIV). As his followers obediently did as Jesus told them, that promise arrived and completely changed the world.

"When the day of Pentecost came, they were all together in one place. Suddenly a sound like the blowing of a violent wind came from heaven and filled the whole house where they were sitting. They saw what seemed to be tongues of fire that separated and came to rest on each of them. All of them were filled with the Holy Spirit and began to speak in other tongues as the Spirit enabled them" (Acts 2:1-4, NIV). This promise is still being fulfilled today.

Fulfillment Makers are filled with the power of the Holy Spirit and carry his flame in their hearts. They allow God's presence to burn hot and bright within them. They learn to trust the Holy Spirit's leading, allowing Him to empower and guide them, and even burn within them, consuming all those deep vulnerabilities. What remains is akin to sparking gold or silver after it's been heated by a refining fire. Impurities are removed and only the purest of the precious metal remains. In the same way, God uses his fire within us to purify and beautify us, transforming us into the best version of ourselves. He accepts us and lovingly refines us to become the very best we can be.

~ The Altar of Blue Fire

Many years ago, I was singing and worshiping the Lord early one Sunday morning before church services began. I was singing "Take Me In" by Integrity's Hosanna! Part of the song lyrics read: "Take me into the Holy of Holies. Take me in by the Blood of the Lamb. Take me into the Holy of Holies. Take the coal, cleanse my lips, here I am." At that moment, I began crying out to God. In John 30:30, John the Baptist mentions, "He must increase and I must decrease." In other words, it means we need to make room for Christ so that he may grow in importance. As I repeated John 30:30 a few times, I remember saying, "NO! NO! Lord, that is not good enough! I want all of You and none of me! All of You and none of me!"

I immediately envisioned myself standing at the foot of a giant burning altar. It was a large bowl, maybe 50 feet in diameter. The flames were dark blue, not like the red flames I was used to seeing in my fireplace. Though I stood at the very edge of this bowl filled with raging, stunningly beautiful blue flames, I saw no wood or coal fueling them. I sensed caution because I knew this fire was consuming everything it touched. As I looked down, I said again, "All of you Lord, none of me!"

Then, suddenly, I was holding my younger brother, Jason, in my arms. Suspended over the inferno, he didn't move; he just dangled in my arms. I looked at his face and his eyes were open, locked and looking right into mine. At that moment, I felt all the incredible love I had for my brother. Next, my brother's face changed instantly and I was now looking into my own face. It was no longer my brother whom I was holding over the flames, but myself.

I recognized all the love I had for myself and an unwillingness to drop myself into these blue flames.

My heart was breaking at the thought of sacrificing this person into the fire. Then, all at once, with utmost compassion, I heard a voice say, "It's harder than you thought, isn't it?" I began to gently weep because of the power of those few words, spoken with great compassion as God's Spirit embraced me. I responded with a short, "Yes, Lord, it is." Then, as fast as it had begun, the vision was over and I was standing up again with my arms open, worshiping.

God's fire is consuming and transforming. It takes away with one hand and gives lavishly with the other. That is how the refiner's fire works within us. The Holy Spirit is compassionate and patient. He understands your vulnerabilities and will gently guide you in his process of consuming transformation. He will guide you to fuel the fire and stoke the flames, one vulnerability at a time.

As we grow to become holders of God's flame, we recognize it's an internal work that produces tremendous outer results. Holders of the flame are infectious to a dying world that needs light and life. We need more people who are burning for God who will not hide the fire. People who burn so brightly with God's light that they eclipse the blinding lights of worldly temptation and set the world ablaze through Christ's passionate heart.

A flame has been prepared and your name is on it. It started burning more than 2000 years ago in that upper room and continues to spread today. It's time to claim the flame of God for your life and be clothed in power from on high. The Holy Spirit is your deposit while you are here on earth. God's plan is for you to be totally equipped with Him. "Where the Spirit of the Lord is, there is freedom" (2 Corinthians 3:17, NIV). Shame has no chain too strong to keep you bound.

You carry the proof to all creation—the seal of the Spirit. It's the only label you will ever need to wear and it marks you as a child of God. Just as you were given royal documents, you were also given a royal seal to prove that you are credible, royal, authentic, and invaluable. With that seal, you carry the authority of the King and all the power of his kingdom within you.

When you say yes to the purposes of God in your life, you are making room for the supernatural power of God to operate in and through you. The Holy Spirit catapults us beyond our own abilities and removes the veil of impossibilities. We live in a new understanding that miracles can break loose at any moment and we wait in hopeful expectation. We begin to understand that we are vessels of blessing that pour the kingdom of God into the same worldly culture that once held us captive. We are blessed to be a blessing; we are healed to become healers. Our chains of captivity were broken so that we might break the chains of others. All of this is done by the power of the Holy

Spirit within us. We are vessels of honor in His eyes and channels of His power. To be a true Shame Breaker and Fulfillment Maker is to be filled with the power from on high.

Be sealed by the Spirit and claim your flame! Pray this prayer with me:

~ Prayer ~

King Jesus, I believe in the promise of your Holy Spirit for my life. According to your glorious riches, I receive this promise and give you thanks. I confess you are the only one who can baptize me with the Holy Spirit and fire. I believe, Holy Spirit, that you are the power from on high. You are the holy fire and I ask you to fill me and clothe me as Jesus said you would. Pour your power out within me and use my life as an instrument of your righteousness. Thank you, Jesus, for your baptism.

Amen.

~ You Carry the Name Above All Names

Proverbs 18:21 ESV tells us that "Death and life are in the power of the tongue, and those who love it will eat its fruit." You carry a very special name in your spiritual backpack. In the previous chapters, I've explained the power of our words. Let's circle back and explore the impact of our word more thoroughly. Imagine again that words are like containers. They always carry something. They can carry life or death. Even empty words contain empty feelings. Based on this understanding, let's examine the meaning of names. If words contain life or death, then names also carry the same force. Word association is a powerful conjurer which can inspire, uplift, and empower … or bring hopelessness, despair, and fragility.

What words do you associate with your name? As mentioned previously, many of us have worn an "ingredients label" listing what the worldly culture says we're made of. We become the product of our mistakes or mistreatments and live in the power of related names. What is your name's container filled with—emptiness … anger … disappointment? As we invite Jesus into our lives, and we're filled with the power of the Holy Spirit, a shift begins to take place. Increasingly, we understand that we aren't the only ones living our lives, but Christ is living in and through us as well. That container of the name of Jesus Christ is now opened and poured into you. It scrubs away the negative graffiti the world has tagged you with and rewrites His name on the walls of your heart. It is from here we must explore the power we have been given in the royal name of Jesus Christ.

This name, Jesus Christ, is packed with everything you need. This truth is best illustrated in the words of the Apostle Paul in Philippians 4:19 (TOT): "I am convinced that my God will fully satisfy every need you have, for I have seen the abundant riches of glory revealed to me through the Anointed One, Jesus Christ!" Jesus is your surplus supply against the lie of scarcity and the fear of not having enough. Yet there is still more to his name—so much more! The name of Jesus is absolute authority, and it's on this topic of authority we will extract the true impact of his name.

Authority is a strong word. It's filled with meaning. "Authority" contains a certain force, perhaps even a certain intimidation. When we talk about authorities, we may rightfully have a sense of respect, maybe a sense of awe, maybe a sense of fear. Authority represents permission. It represents power and symbolizes rule, control, and influence. When someone has authority, that means they're on top of a hierarchy of other individuals or organizations. They have responsibility beyond what is normal. They are able to determine things, to decide things, to render judgments, and to wield certain rights and actions.

Matthew 28:18 (ESV) tells us: "And Jesus came and said to them, 'All authority in heaven and on earth has been given to me.'" In the framework of this passage, Jesus is saying He is at the top of creation's hierarchy, which includes everything in heaven and on earth. Many bible translations refer to his office of authority as King of Kings and Lord of Lords.

Luke 10:17-22 ESV says: "The seventy-two returned with joy and said, 'Lord, even the demons submit to us in your name.' He replied, 'I saw Satan fall like lightning from heaven. I have given you authority to trample on snakes and scorpions and to overcome all the power of the enemy; nothing will harm you. However, do not rejoice that the spirits submit to you, but rejoice that your names are written in heaven.' At that time Jesus, full of joy through the Holy Spirit, said, 'I praise you, Father, Lord of heaven and earth, because you have hidden these things from the wise and learned, and revealed them to little children. Yes, Father, for this is what you were pleased to do. All things have been committed to me by my Father.'"

This same authority has been given to you to overcome all the Enemy's power. The name of Jesus is your family name. As a Christ-follower, your name is written in the Lamb's Book of Life. In terms of genealogy, you don't need to pay for a DNA test; you are in the family tree of God! The authority invested in the name of your king is invested in your name now—not the name shame gave you, but the living name of God.

Notice Jesus said not to rejoice because, in his authority, we are destroying the works of the Enemy. Rather, we are to rejoice because we are family. Authority is a natural byproduct of being a child of God. You are an ambassador of the king. We bring His kingdom with us everywhere we go. This is reflected in 2 Corinthians 5:20 and in Luke 17:21, when Jesus mentioned that the kingdom of God is carried inside of us. We wear his name and shame has no hold over us any longer. His name was given as a free gift of grace. Upon receiving this gift, we can begin to view everything differently.

I have control and absolute authority in Christ Jesus. This empowering truth has helped me overcome shame during some of my toughest battles. As believers, we all have this same resource within us to bring along the atmosphere of God's throne room, everywhere we go and in every situation we face. Our Jesus is an extravagant giver, even to the point of sharing his throne with you right this very moment. If Christians could see things through Christ's heavenly perspective—far above all other authorities and dominions—and recognize that, by the Holy Spirit, we are seated in Christ, we would begin to realize the meaning of Jesus' words more fully when he said, "Greater is He who is in you than he who is in the world." (John 4:4 BSB) **The secret weapon to our warfare is knowing the atmosphere in you is greater than the atmosphere around you.**

What does atmosphere mean in this context? It is the throne-room atmosphere of Almighty God. The Apostle Paul wrote of this in Ephesians 2:6-7 (NIV): "And God raised us up with Christ and seated us with him in the heavenly realms in Christ Jesus, in order that in the coming ages he might show the incomparable riches of his grace, expressed in his kindness to us in Christ Jesus." Notice, Paul does not say "*when you go to heaven*, you are seated with Christ." He says God already has "raised us up." That is past tense, meaning it has already happened!

Let's examine these next four Scriptures for greater insight. Fulfillment Makers recognize who they are in Christ and live out each day from that throne-room advantage.

1 Peter 3:22 (ESV): "Who has gone into heaven and is at the right hand of God, with angels, authorities, and powers having been subjected to him."

Romans 8:34 (ESV): "Who is to condemn? Christ Jesus is the one who died—more than that, who was raised—who is at the right hand of God, who indeed is interceding for us."

Colossians 3:1 (ESV): "If then you have been raised with Christ, seek the things that are above, where Christ is, seated at the right hand of God."

Hebrews 12:2 (ESV): "Looking to Jesus, the founder and perfecter of our faith, who for the joy that was set before him endured the cross, despising the shame, and is seated at the right hand of the throne of God."

These truths explain part of the wonderful exchange of the finished work of Christ—from having zero authority to having absolute authority ... from having no position of victory to being seated in absolute victory.

Ask a military strategist where the best place to fight from is, and they will likely say the high ground. Similarly, you have the ultimate vantage point from where you are seated in Christ. The view is amazing from here. The moment Jesus took his seat on the throne, he brought you with him. This privilege revolutionizes everything. Once we begin to see every situation, every crisis, every problem, and every outlook from the most high place, everything else looks small.

So often, we view our battles and difficulties *from* the ground position. We pray from the vantage point of our problems rather than praying from the throne-room reality. There is a huge difference between these two fighting positions. Where you choose to fight your battles from makes all the difference in the outcome and the casualties inflicted—and sustained— in any war. The divine exchange, from defeat to victory, has already been accomplished. When you realize God strategically positioned you for victory, you partake in Christ's overcomer mindset. The Devil doesn't know what to do with a person who lives life from the throne-room perspective.

Historically, warriors have always attempted to conquer and camp on the high ground. Doing so gave them a superior view of their enemy and enabled those on the high ground to anticipate attacks and plan accordingly. It was also exhausting for the enemy to have to climb in order to attack, zapping them of their strength before the fight. A high-ground strategy also ensured the sun was facing the camp's rearguard. This served two purposes: It helped improved visibility where, otherwise, pockets of darkness could conceal attackers, and it forced attackers to fight facing into the sun, blinding them during the battle.

In the same way, we are seated with Christ at the right hand of God. He is shining over us, exposing the Enemy with clear visibility. He shines so brightly that our enemies are blinded. It is in this place, seated in Christ Jesus, that the darkness can be fully exposed and angel armies and the mighty power of the Holy Spirit are unleashed. Our willingness to be vulnerable and obedient to do God's will allows us to share in Jesus' strategic dominance, authority, and power. As a result, we deliver ourselves and others by defeating the Enemy, who comes to "steal, kill and destroy" (John 10:10).

Your birthright is to live this victorious life now, through the power and authority of Christ, and to release the victory "on earth as it is in heaven." That is your calling! That is your assignment! Shame Breakers and Fulfillment Takers partner with God's kingdom, changing the landscape of our lives and others', and releasing the throne-room atmosphere that is inside us into the world around us.

Does this mean Jesus is a genie in a bottle? Of course not. God's miracle is in the process—not just the destination. His priority is your transformation, which requires you to roll up your sleeves and do the hard work. You must depend on His strength and power throughout the process. It's from these battles that your character will be forged. If battles were not full of conflict, they would not be called battles. But each battle won is a monument of praise to God and a boost of all types of good things you give to yourself.

We also need to understand that failure is an unavoidable part of God's process and is even necessary in order to develop our fullest potential and greatest fulfillment. We *will* fail and lose the fight at times, but we have not lost the battle. In these most discouraging moments, we must remain focused, shake off the dust, and sit enthroned with the promised victory in mind (Isaiah 52:2). Learn from mishaps and continue to grow from them. The Devil can't beat a person who just won't quit! Keep trusting in the One who went before you to pave the way to your promised victory. "The One who calls you is faithful, and He will do it" (1Thessalonians, 5:24).

~ Working with the Father

One of my fondest childhood memories was going to work with my dad. I was about 5 years old the first time. In those days, he worked in the oil fields as a heavy equipment operator. One piece of equipment he drove was a giant earth mover, designed to clear and level large sections of land with its large front-end blade. I remember approaching this monster of a machine with my dad. It looked larger than our house with a chair right in the middle. To gain entry, Dad had to climb an on-board ladder while carrying me with one arm gripped around my waist.

I remember, as we got to the top, where the seat was located, I could see all the way to the ocean marina. The view was amazing from that spot. I felt like I was on the top of a skyscraper. My dad seated me with him, pointing out that he had to clear out all the black oil sludge from the entire area. I could see it all around us, like stacks of gross, black jellyfish. Through my eyes, the task looked impossible. Then he said, "Tony, you're going to do it! You're going to drive the earth mover and clear the land of this sludge." I was nervous and excited at the same time. He fired up the monster machine and revved the engine which began to rumble and shake everything. I was rattling so much that I couldn't speak normally! Even my vocal cords were shaking with the power of this machine.

"Don't worry, I will help you," my dad said while explaining how to pull the levers to turn the behemoth right and left, and how to raise and lower the front blade. Unbeknownst to me, he did all the work that day. I was just seated with him. While my little hands seemed to be pulling those levers, my dad actually had his hand on top of mine, giving me the needed strength. It is one of my greatest childhood memories— a time of bonding, and yet a time of transforming a landscape from gross sludge to clean, smooth ground.

Similarly, I believe being seated in Christ is not much different. God does the work but allows our little hands to get involved. We shift and transform landscapes, removing what is harmful to create clean, smooth ground. Ridding ourselves of shame seems, at times, like an impossible task. Its residual sludge ruins everything and cleaning it requiring an incredible amount of tireless effort. But the process brings the greatest blessing of intimacy with Christ that we can ever experience. There is so much available for you as a child of the king. He desires to share all He has with you.

What a great way to close this powerful story of Mephibosheth. I pray that it inspires you to reject the mouth of shame and the prison into which it has locked you. It's time to rise up, shake off the rubble and debris from past battles, and sit enthroned with your heavenly Father. Allow the King to set you free and give you a new life as one of his children seated at his table of plenty. Be the Shame Breaker and Fulfillment Taker in your world today.

~ Prayer ~

Lord Jesus, I praise you that all authority and positioning of yourself has already been shared with me. I receive it with such thankfulness and gratitude, knowing you paid the highest price for me to share in your victory. Enlighten my understanding that I am victorious in you. In Jesus Name!

Amen.

Name the Shame — It Has an Itchy Trigger Finger

"Anyone a you lily-livered, bow-legged varmints care to slap leather with me, in case any of you git ideas you better know who you're dealin' with. I'm Yosemite Sam. The roughest, toughest, he-man stuffest hombre as ever crossed the Rio Grande … and I ain't no namby-pamby."

~ Yosemite Sam
(*American Looney Toons Cartoon Character*)

We all have shame triggers that provoke a reflexive reaction when our pain button is pushed. It's vital to be conscious of when those buttons are activated, noticing how we react and the warning signs our body gives us. When shame is triggered, three severe, negative feelings can cripple us:

1. The feeling of being trapped
2. The feeling of being worthless
3. The feeling of being powerless

Any of these feelings, by themselves, can create a powerful emotional storm. But when activated simultaneously, the result is like a devastating tornado that leaves nothing but destruction in its path. These three feelings have a tendency to erupt very quickly and without warning. They have an uncanny ability to hijack our reasoning skills. Instead, we may respond with an adrenaline rush of toxic emotions.

As a survivor of toxic shame, myself, at one point in my healing process, I realized that my emotions didn't always cooperate with the rational part of my mind. Being triggered felt like being hotwired—revved up and ready to go. It was as if I were just a passenger along for the ride with someone else in the driver's seat. If you can identify with my experience, I want to reassure you that you're not alone. This reaction is simply our human nature at work, reflecting how shame operates in us on a physiological level.

In moments like these, it's important to remember: **greater is the Holy Spirit at work in us than the shame that is working against us!** Shame, in many ways, is like post-traumatic stress. It tries to hide in our bodies. For example, my arms and face tingle when my shame button is pushed. Others, when their triggers are activated, may notice tension in their lower jaw and their face becoming flushed. Still others say their hands become sweaty, and they get tunnel vision. The body serves as an alarm system when the core parts of who we are become threatened. It sends a distress signal. When this occurs, it's important to recognize the pain and immediately confront it.

One way I handle my body's physical reaction to shame is by attaching a humorous label to it. Humor, I've found, often helps me regain control of my emotions. For example, when I feel the physical symptoms beginning, I picture Yosemite Sam, the Looney Tunes cartoon character. He is commonly depicted as an extremely aggressive, gunslinging, outlaw with a hair-trigger temper and an intense hatred of his nemesis, Bugs Bunny. Like Yosemite Sam—also known for his grumpy demeanor, harsh voice, and short stature—if I'm being honest, he accurately depicts how I can act when I feel trapped, worthless, or powerless. When our bodies are thrown into a chaotic storm, it's normal to feel small as we recall, if only subconsciously, the smallness we've felt in our past.

When shame strikes, we typically respond in one of two ways: In an attempt to win acceptance, we puff up like a puffer fish and pretend to be bigger, better, and stronger than the one who is making us feel small. Or, we shrink our essence to become smaller— a person hidden in plain sight—pleasing others to win acceptance at the cost of discarding healthy boundaries and self-worth. No matter which approach we take, the common theme is the feeling of smallness.

I remember at my workplace, years back, a new boss began heading our department. For the purposes of this story, I will call him BK. As far as I was concerned, he was a brilliant master of pushing my shame buttons. This guy had the ability to turn my spectacular day into an absolute shame-fest in a blink of an eye! I remember the first sales call BK and I made together, where I gave a presentation to executives of a large manufacturing company. Audience members were engaged and communicative. By the end of my presentation, we won the contract and company leaders made a verbal offer to move forward.

I walked to my car feeling like I was on cloud nine, while replaying the client's enthusiastic "yes" over and over in my mind. Suddenly, my solo soiree was interrupted by a voice coming from a car in the parking spot near me. It was BK.

"Tony, jump in my car. I want to talk with you and debrief the meeting," he said.

As soon as I was seated, BK asked abruptly, "How did you feel the meeting went?"

"It went great!" I replied enthusiastically. "We won the contract! They seemed very excited to join with us!"

That's when the party ended.

"I felt your presentation lacked depth, and you could have elaborated much more on the features and benefits of our product and services."

At that moment, my face began to tingle. It was my body's alarm going off, telling me Yosemite Sam was about to make his grand entrance, guns ablaze. Sure enough, before I could even take my next breath, I fired off a snippy response.

"Did you not read the customer file? We already had two meetings prior to this one regarding the specifications of the product and services. The clients already are thoroughly familiar with the system operations!"

War broke out in the front seat of BK's Mini Cooper. He fired a heated volley in my direction, asserting that my presentation skills lacked depth. I unleashed the heavy artillery via a fiery come-back: "I'm very surprised you're saying this because I was awarded top salesman of the year, beating out the other two-thousand sales-team members nationwide!" Then, I added, "The company pays me to train other sales members to do exactly what you witnessed in action today. So, apparently, I must be doing something right."

We spent the next couple minutes shooting up the place. By the time we were finished, we each bore more holes in our imaginary armor than swiss cheese. About 20 minutes later, on my drive home, however, a tsunami of regret swept over me. I began to pray and ask God to forgive me. I knew I'd been operating from a place of shame. I realized BK's remarks had left me feeling small and inadequate. My response was to puff up and fight.

My ego is such a prima donna. When it feels small, it fights back with an inflated view of my own importance. I had been praying over the months leading up to this incident that the Lord would teach me how to break off this area of shame in my life. As I recognized the embarrassment of acting like a prima donna, I also realized God was using BK to sculpt me into the person I needed to become. **Sometimes, God will send hand-picked people into your life to act as his divine chisel to shape you into a better version of yourself.** People *will* push your shame button, but rely on and ask the Holy Spirit to help you learn from it and grow.

We become stronger through experiencing resistance, just as muscles are strengthened and grow through resistance-training with weights. In other words, some relationships might carry a little more resistance. In those instances, we need to ask ourselves an important question. Will this be a teaching moment to grow from, or should I walk away because the confrontation level is just too high and unhealthy? It's not always an easy question to answer.

In the case of my relationship with BK, it was short-lived. I resigned from my position and moved on in my career. Even so, I learned more about myself and how I react to shame triggers. I took another step in my healing process by recognizing the warning signs of when my emotions are hotwiring and wanting to take control. I also became fed up with the regret I would inevitably experience after such moments, which motivated me towards much-needed change.

Even today, in my current stage of life, I have shame triggers. But now I can say to myself, "That's hitting my shame button and Yosemite Sam's not going to help the situation by shooting up the place. Let's holster those guns, take a break, and regroup." Removing myself, quickly and professionally, from flammable environments, then coming back when calmer emotions prevail, is the secret. It takes *a lot* of practice, lots of prayer, and even specific skills to master this maneuver. Though it's tempting to run from shame triggers, I now know that doing so would only stunt my growth and ability to evolve.

In our harder moments, there are a few things that can help beat shame flair-ups. It is worth mentioning again that God will put people in your life that are the chisel in his hand to help sculpt you into the best version of yourself, and eventually, reflect the wonderful expressions of Jesus Christ. We cannot run from the chisel when it is in God's hand.

~ Prayer ~

Lord, in those moments I lose myself ... I thank you that you never lose me. Help me to grow and evolve from those moments when I get caught off guard from shame. Give me the strength and the self-control that comes from your Spirit to subdue it in your power.

Amen.

Battle Tactics for Breaking the Mouth of Shame

"Take God at His Word—because winning the battle doesn't require physical brawn, but spiritual brains!"
~ Pedro Okoro

I want to equip you with tactics I've adopted over the years to help me win the battle against shame. When shame is triggered and an attack is in progress, these "battle tactics" can make all the difference.

~ Listen to Your Body, Mind, and Emotions

Jesus told his disciples to "watch and pray." It is from this lesson that we learn we must constantly be vigilant. Learn to be in tune with your body, mind, and emotions. Pay close attention to what your whole self is telling you. When it comes to the mind, you must begin to make time as Joyce Meyer, author of *Battlefield of the Mind*, would say, "Think about what you are thinking about." Remember that your mind is fertile and whatever seed you agree with will grow, take root, and bear fruit. Good fruit produces good things and bad fruit produces poison. When the mouth of shame speaks, we must take it captive and expel it from our minds in the powerful name of Jesus. Emotions at times can hotwire our bodies, bypassing our minds altogether. Learn to be sensitive to the physical symptoms within your body when emotions begin to flare. Pay attention to whatever thoughts and feelings begin to rise up within you. Note any physical sensations. Notice what you say or do when you feel this way. Notice what happens around you or how it affects others when you are feeling this way.

Listening to your body, mind, and emotions is a way to acknowledge that your shame trigger has been activated. Avoiding, minimizing, blaming, and refusing to actively resist shame only creates theft, death, and destruction in your life. Own your shame triggers. They're yours and nobody else's. That's why you're the only one who can deal with them. Ask the Holy Spirit to help you identify and discern if shame is striking out against you. If it is, begin praying right away within your mind and with all your heart. He knows your thoughts and is available to help you in your moment of need.

~ Face It and Fight It

Once you know shame is on the attack, face it head on and stand your ground. The warrior in you must rise up and fight. The fuel for the fight must come from the Holy Spirit's supernatural power, love, and anointing working inside you. The Bible says "perfect love casts out fear" (1 John 4:18, ESV). Love yourself as God loves you and, from that place of strength, wage war against shame. Look it in its eyes, go nose to nose, and tell it NO! You must refuse it. You must declare to shame that you are no longer willing to follow its lead. When shame tries to chain you to the fear of not measuring up, you must take authority and control by naming shame before it names you. You must force it to wear your label and not the other way around. Remind it that "greater is He who is in you than he who is in the world" (1 John 4:4, BSB).

As I've shared, Yosemite Sam is the name I use for my shame trigger reactions. Why do I do that? It is actually a technique therapists use in narrative therapy, called "externalization." For me, having a funny name for my reaction lessens my tension, and it also isolates the shame emotions from my authentic self rather than having shame isolate me. It gives me the advantage of knowing **I'm not shame and shame is not me,** separating its attachment to me.

Shame will always try to convince you it's part of you and who you are, but it's not. It is only a hitchhiker that's trying to catch a ride. Don't take it with you! It's at this point, you call it by name, and say, in the name of Jesus, "I reject you and refuse you. Leave at once from my mind, will, and my emotions. Go! Go! Go!"

You must remember where you are seated (on the throne) as you speak this command. You must remember whose child and family you belong to (the King of Kings and Lord of Lords). You must remember the power of the Holy Spirit, the down payment of the glorious riches of Jesus Christ, who has been given to you. You have more than enough and you are enough. Use all of your resources to your advantage. Beat shame into submission in Jesus' name. There is nothing in of all creation that can separate you from the love of God. No angels or demons, nor principalities, nor powers … nothing in this age or the age to come can defeat the love God has for you (Romans 8:38-39). You have the absolute victory in Jesus' mighty name.

~ Vulnerability

Vulnerability with Jesus always leads to the impartation of blessings. In moments when the fight is on, we must be true to ourselves and accept our flaws and vulnerabilities so that we can be healed. If we hide and ignore our flaws, we will never become a Shame Breaker and Fulfillment Maker. Healing and receiving

God's restoring touch and forgiveness always comes through the gate of vulnerability.

Verbally confess those areas where you feel inadequate. When we come to him authentically, with all our vulnerabilities exposed, he is loving and gracious. In all honesty, that is what true repentance is all about. By faith, we share our flaws with him, trusting that we're accepted, healed, and set free by the power of Jesus Christ. Ask Jesus to heal you and set you free. Let the Holy Spirit guide you and bring you into peace and restoration.

Many times, in these situations, he will bring rest to your mind and peace to the chaotic emotions violently crashing inside of you. He can settle the storm. He will also reveal things that perhaps you were not aware of about the circumstances you are dealing with, and give you wisdom and insight to handle them. Let the Holy Spirit fill with life and fulfillment the gaping voids that shame once occupied. Only he can.

This is also a time to pick up the Word of God— the Bible. Affirm the promises of how God sees you and hold onto them. Form agreements with them and let the good fruit of the Spirit grow in your life. There are many online studies of the love of God and His promises and blessings. Use those and keep them nearby. You will find them to be powerful tools when battling shame.

~ Healthy Circle of Trust

Reach out to a trusted confidant and share your story with them. Belonging to a healthy circle of trusted people must be a priority. James 5:16 says that, as we confess our sin to one another and pray for each other, healing comes into our lives. I believe our vulnerabilities are also healed through open communication with a loving friend who is willing to journey and pray with you. We are created by God to be relational, connected beings. Humanity is at its weakest when isolated from others. Our sweet spot of fulfillment is found at the center of belonging. It is imperative for our happiness that we have healthy relationships.

This is why Satan has always worked so hard to destroy relationships. In fact, it is his only purpose and strategy, as I mentioned earlier. It is imperative that you work diligently to build a healthy circle of people who have earned the right to be trusted with your vulnerabilities. This inner circle should be composed of people who don't throw stones of shame … people with whom you can talk openly and honestly, without having to wear a mask. These are the kind of people who will not always say what you want to hear. Instead, they will speak, in love, what is needed. They are the people who are capable of going the distance … friends who will still be by your side—loving boundaries in place—when you drop a bombshell and the dust settles.

I know first-hand that it's not easy to let people get close when we're mired in shame. The fear of rejection is always a battle. **Even so, small, steady strides can lead to huge healing.** In Christian circles, this can be very difficult because of the religious spirit that influences many. Sadly, the law is more dominant in some hearts than the grace and love of Jesus Christ. Just because a person claims to be a Christian, doesn't mean they have earned the right to be part of your inner circle. Test the spirits of people and extend trust a little at a time. As trust is earned and honored, more can be shared. Pray that God would lead you into healthy relationships that will help you to grow, not weigh you down.

If Jesus, being the Son of God, needed his inner circle—Peter, James and John—then how much more do you need yours? Healthy relationships should always be valued and never discounted. We all need to belong. Reach out to a friend in the times of struggle. Pray together and get that healthy dose of belonging and acceptance.

~ Intentional Love

Fulfillment Makers use their whole heart, especially from their wounded places, to love extravagantly. They know love rejects all forms of selfishness, including the use of another for one's own fulfillment. They reject the idea of "playing games" in relationships because they do not seek to manipulate. Instead, they seek to accept others as they truly are—no mask required. They have same the whole-hearted approach to love that Jesus taught: "Love the Lord, your God, with all your heart, with all your soul, and with all your mind; and with all your strength; and your neighbor as yourself" (Luke 10:27, NIV).

Loving your neighbor as you would like to be loved raises the question: How can I best love others? How you treat another person will reveal to them whether or not they matter to you. But if you don't love yourselves and value yourself, it will be difficult to love others to any beneficial degree. The first step of loving intentionally, then, is to love yourself as Christ loves you. Respect yourself. Treat yourself with kindness. Forgive yourself and embrace your flaws and imperfections.

As we begin loving others from the healed wounds of our past—from that place where God first met us—God can use us to facilitate someone else's healing because we know what it's like to have those same wounds and experiences (2 Cor 1:4). If you wish to love intentionally, look in your mirror and realize that you are wonderfully made. From that place of understanding, you can begin to see the same in others around you. Our motivation for how we treat people should always flow from the love God has for us individually. Only then can we bring that love to others. Actions really do speak louder than words, and your actions have the power to communicate love more convincingly than just telling someone that you love them.

As followers of Christ, we should strive to always treat others with love. We should always fight spiritual battles with love. It is what we were created for as sons and daughters, made in the image and likeness of love. Be intentional every day to do random acts of kindness toward others. Let your light shine and be the healing to someone else's pain through the heart of Jesus Christ.

As you love others intentionally, you'll realize that you also will grow in love for yourself. You might not have a whole lot of self-love to begin with, but that's OK. Use what you do have now—spend it on yourself and others—and, in time, your love will grow. When Jesus said to love others as yourself, he meant just that. We can't just say, "Well, first I need to love myself and, until that happens, I can't love others." Heavens no! Spend whatever measure of love you have in your heart today. This is the way of growing in love, holding nothing back.

There's no such thing as a love savings plan! It's a spending plan! The more you spend, the more you get; and the more you hold back, the less you receive. Regardless of how much love you have now, I challenge you to intentionally spend it all. In fact, it's in the midst of a shame attack that you must spend your love currency all the more, because nothing brings worth and destroys fear more than love.

~ Fulfillment Taker 10 ~

Prayer of Freedom and Filling

*"Our prayers may be awkward. Our attempts may
be feeble. But since the power of prayer is in the
one who hears it and not in the one who says it,
our prayers do make a difference.""*

~ Max Lucado

Think of every bit of knowledge, understanding
or affirmation that you've learned from this book
to this point as seeds. These seeds—plus everything
you hold in your memory, which forms agreements
with the seeds—combine to form revelation. In this
final chapter, it's now time to ask God, the Father of
our Lord Jesus Christ, to continue to water, making
the seeds of life grow, and producing in you good
fruit. Perhaps you have lived life battling a painful
harvest of bad seeds. It's time now, through prayer, to
allow God to access the garden of your whole being.

When you do this, something supernatural
happens and the power of God moves upon the

wholehearted prayers of His children. And, yes, you are His child! This is the moment, by faith, I believe He is going to root out of your heart's garden old belief systems and agreements that have hindered you from being fulfilled. He is going to prune some areas to make room for new growth, and He is going to plant new things that will create a beautiful landscape in your life. He is bringing newness of life, and I am so overwhelmed with joy to see, through the eyes of faith, you overcome.

We know from Revelations 12:11 that this over-coming occurs by the "blood of the Lamb," Jesus Christ, and the words of your testimony—the unique story of what He is doing in your life. The only requirement of you is simply to be willing to let Him in and partner with you in this life-changing work. Being willing to be willing is a very simple concept. It means wholeheartedly coming to Christ with whatever you have in your hand right now.

A great example is David. He slayed Goliath, but not with a huge sword or even a spear. No, he used what was in his hand—a plain, small rock that killed the giant on the spot. The Goliath of shame might look huge as you face it on your emotional battlefield but remember: God will use what is in your hand, no matter how plain or small, to slay that beast.

Sometimes, we feel the only way we can experience real breakthrough is by wielding a case full of weaponry to fight off the Enemy. In other words, we think we need to reach some level of power and perfection to have victory. It's interesting that the kingdom of God is not like that at all. As was the case with David and Goliath, God uses the *least* expected things, the *last* of all the acclaimed things, to totally annihilate the Enemy.

Right now, say this to yourself:

"I am qualified! I am accepted! I am approved through Jesus Christ!"

Let him guide your shaky hands to use what you carry now to become a Shame Breaker and Fulfillment Maker.

This battle begins with the intimacy and full acceptance you have in Christ. From the heart of Christ, there is a unique anointing, a supernatural power, that empties us of shame and pours in its place God's individual recipe of fulfillment from the Holy Spirit. This is a moment of a loving encounter between you and God. Get alone. Set aside some time and have an encounter with the King at His table. I pray your experience is overwhelming as you taste and see the Lord is good. There is no sin, shame, or wrongdoing that is more powerful than the grace and love of Jesus Christ. As Ezekiel 37:1-14 declares, the dry bones of your life are about to awaken again! Hallelujah, hallelujah, hallelujah!

~ Invitational Prayer

Picture your heart as a home and Jesus is at the door knocking. You open the door and invite Him in as you pray the following prayer. Let Him wander, giving Him total approval to go inside every room, every closet—yes, even every drawer! As you pray, He might bring various situations to your mind. Even though it might feel scary or overwhelming, be strong and allow yourself push through ... you're doing great! Let Him lead you to hand over your vulnerable spots— your pains and inadequacies. His love is the gift he brings as He enters into your heart to live with you.

Please pray this out loud ...

"I call out to you, Lord Jesus, because I know you will hear me. I call out your name, Jesus, because only you will set me free from the curse of sin and shame. There is ultimate power in your name, Jesus. I speak your name over everything that opposes God's blessings in my life. I call out your name from the deepest places of my heart. Come in like a flood and move upon my life. Let the waves of your presence wash over me as your word says in Psalm 42:7.

"Come, Lord Jesus!

"Move in Power, Lord Jesus!

"Overtake me, Lord Jesus!

"Every solution begins and ends with you at work within me. I partner with you now. I form a healthy

agreement, based on your promise, that there is no power in all of creation that can separate me from the love of God (Romans 8:38).

"I call upon your name, because EVERYONE who calls upon the name of the Lord, will be saved (Romans 10:13)!

"You're the way, the truth, and the life, and no one comes to the Father except through you (John 14-6).

"Here and now, I affix myself to the eternal agreement made with the blood of Jesus Christ, the Son of the Living God, granting me complete and eternal salvation. I declare openly before God, my Father, that I choose you, Jesus, to be the Lord of my life. I declare you are the flawless Lamb of God and your blood has purchased my freedom from the curse of sin and shame. Today and forever, my soul stands firm in the absolute, unbreakable promise of your love and acceptance toward me.

"I open the door of my heart and ask you to come inside. My heart is your home … I give it to you. I give you complete access to every area, even the places I've hidden from myself and others. Jesus, I surrender and ask you to remove what must be removed. Make room within me for your kingdom. I want your good and perfect will to be done in my life. I share with you every vulnerability in my life—all the mistakes, all the deep wounds, and every pain. Touch the broken areas of my life, healing me and making me whole. I trust in You *and I choose life and reject death. I heap all my sin upon You, believing that You took them all with You when You died on the cross two thousand years ago. I ask You now to do a deep work in my life. Demolish every stronghold and bring to my mind each habit, word, and deed that must die by being nailed to your cross.*

In Your matchless name, Jesus, amen."

As you pray, take your time and don't rush. Be still, quiet your spirit, and notice what the Lord is doing. Let God lighten your load. Allow yourself time to feel Him removing the heavy stones in your spiritual backpack. Allow Him to meander through your heart's landscape with you. Let Him bring things up—those areas you hide from everyone else, maybe even yourself. Let Him tenderly touch your wounds and begin to heal them. Once you sense this time of prayer is over, move on to the Prayer of Agreement, below. You might feel that you need to repeat these prayers often at first, and that's okay. Just know you have the blessed assurance of salvation, you do not need to get resaved daily.

~ Prayer of Agreement ~

Please pray the following prayer out loud:

"In the name of Jesus, I break the powers of shame in my life! I command the dream of God to come alive

within me. I declare that, though I have been struck down, I will not be destroyed. I declare I am risen in the power of the Holy Spirit at work in me. I declare, in Jesus' name, to myself, that I will rise up and live in the fulfillment of the promises of God!

"By the power of God's Spirit within, I break every chain that shame has produced in my life. In the name of Jesus, I cast off all inherited rejection that has been passed down to me by my ancestors and the culture of this world. I forgive myself and those who have passed shame down to me. I reject the poison of unforgiveness in my heart. I set myself free, in Jesus name, from all entanglements with the roots of bitterness. I cast off all defilements they have created in my life.

"Every false agreement, I break and cast off completely from my life in the mighty name of Jesus! I receive and make new agreements within myself through the heart of Jesus Christ. I agree with God that I am wonderful and loved by Him. I agree with God that all my sins and mistakes are under the blood of Jesus and I accept the fact that I am forgiven. I agree with God that all those sins and mistakes are remembered no more by Him. As it is with Him, so it shall be with me … forgiven and forgotten under the blood of Jesus!

"I reject all lies that say I am not worthy of love. In Jesus' mighty name, I break the lies of unworthiness. I *disavow and deny the mouth of shame … its voice has no power over me!*

"*In Jesus' name, I break the mouth of shame that speaks against me.*

"*In Jesus' name, I evict that voice of shame out of my life. GO! GO! GO!*

"*I declare I am emptied of shame and I praise you, Jesus, for the freedom and liberty through your Holy Spirit. Jesus, only you baptize with the Holy Spirit and fire. Today, I form an agreement within myself because you qualified me to receive it. I ask you now for the infilling of the baptism of the Holy Spirit in my life.*

"*Holy Spirit, come! In Jesus' matchless name!*

"*Build your kingdom within me and use me to be a Shame Breaker and Fulfillment Maker. Bless me to be a blessing, that I may overflow with your Holy Spirit's power, to bring you glory with my life. I ask that your courageous love and holy fire burn hot within me, bringing the kingdom of heaven everywhere I go. To you be the kingdom, the power, and the glory forever and ever in Jesus' mighty name, amen!*"

Praise Him for your victory!

I am exceedingly proud of you for beginning the hard steps of overcoming what the Devil meant for your harm. You are now partnered with God, the Author of your life. You can now begin to write a new story together with Him—one meant to prosper you in every way.

Though this book is finished, your own story is not. A page has been turned and a new chapter is just beginning. As you begin this new chapter, walking in the increased power of the Holy Spirit, I leave you with this simple quote:

"God will always call you by your abilities, while shame will always call you by your disabilities."
~ Tony Caiazza, Evangelist

"Be strong and courageous. Never forget that in Christ you are a Shame Breaker and Fulfillment Taker!"

In Memory of:

Bob Evans
Thank you for teaching me that it's okay to be the
bull in the Devil's china closet, and ….
not to step in the oil!

Sheri Gering
Thank you for showing me that the
only perception that carries any weight
is the perception that God has of me.

About the Author

Tony Caiazza is an international evangelist who delivers high energy messages that challenge audiences to refocus and reset their thinking to what matters most in life. Unlocking God's full potential for both individuals and organizations has been his calling for many years. Audiences love his practical strategies on breaking shame and fear mindsets. Tony's life story of hardships and triumphs have culminated from a mixed blend of experiences as a pastor, evangelist, and entrepreneur, and continues to encourage thousands.

Tony and his wife Angela own Fulfillment Family Therapy, a mental health practice dedicated to helping others reach their full potential.

For over a decade, their practice has helped others to overcome challenging circumstances and obtain true healing. It is from these experiences Tony has carefully curated the twenty steps to being a Shame Breaker and Fulfillment Taker. His faith in Jesus Christ and dependence on the power of the Holy

Spirit aligns God's breakthrough to forever change lives.

Tony values the connection he has with his readers and attendees at his seminars. To inquire about him speaking at your next event or group meeting, or to join him on social media, you can contact him through e-mail:

info@shame-breakers.com

or find him at:

www.tonycaiazza.com

@shamebreakers

https://www.facebook.com/shamebreakers